TREADMILL WORKOUTS

90 Treadmill Workouts For Every Runner

AMY BEATTY

Treadmill Workouts: 90 Treadmill Workouts For Every Runner.

Amy Beatty.
Published by Rockville Publishing

Cover Design: ASEL Productions

ISBN: 978-1515301622

"Running teaches me that I am capable of so much more than I ever imagined. "

TABLE OF CONTENTS

DISCLAIMER

The writers of Treadmill Workouts strongly recommend that you consult with your physician before beginning any exercise program. You should be in good physical condition and be able to participate in the exercise.

The writers of Treadmill Workouts are not a licensed medical care provider and represent no expertise in diagnosing, examining, or treating medical conditions of any kind, or in determining the effect of any specific exercise on a medical condition.

You should understand that when participating in any exercise or exercise program, there is the possibility of physical injury. If you engage in this exercise or exercise program, you agree that you do so at your own risk, are voluntarily participating in these activities, assume all risk of injury to yourself, and agree to release and discharge the writers and publishers of Treadmill Workouts from any and all claims or causes of action, known or unknown, arising out of Treadmill Workouts negligence.

FORWARD

I'VE HATED RUNNING. I've loved running. I've been good and I've been really bad. I've set records. I've nearly keeled over after being lapped by the majority of the race field, finding myself fighting with everything I had, not to wind up in last place. I've hallucinated on runs and been totally disoriented from the relentless summer heat. I've felt my teeth chattering in the bitterness of winter, swearing that one of my toes were surely lost to hypothermia on the run.

I've run for trophies. I've run for glory. I've run for records and for prize money. I've raced distances from the 400 meters to the marathon (and everything in between). I've run to qualify to this or that. But I've also run to escape heartache. I've run with tears streaming down my face, mile after mile. I've run on treadmills, sidewalks, roads, trails, beaches and up windy mountain hills. I've run when I've been somebody and I've run when I've been nobody. And I keep running because...I am a runner.

Running has taught me that the harder you work, the more successful you become. Running has also taught me that lactic acid is very real. I've learned that there's a reason why we run the race; you never know who will win on *that* day because the only thing that's sure in this world is change. I've learned that you know you're a runner when you pay attention to the color of your urine- it's a free hydration monitor. And I am still learning countless life lessons as I continue to run. I watch movies when I run on the treadmill. I listen to music, loud. If I'm running on a treadmill at the gym, I can't help but race the runner next to me; I swear competitiveness is in my DNA. When I run on the treadmill I know I'm going to get a great workout. I'm not interrupted from traffic crossing my path, I'm not trudging through a foot of snow or trying to keep my balance on patches of ice. I'm exactly where I want to be. On a treadmill. Is it lonely running on a treadmill? Sometimes, yes. But I surround myself with movies, good music and I always remind myself of my goal(s). I am training with an intention. Whether it's to stay healthy or to run a personal best time in my next race, I always run with a purpose.

I bet you've had times when you've hated running, too. Then again, I bet you've had plenty of times when you've loved it. It's all part of being a runner. If you're new to running- welcome! There's nothing quite like the support of the running community. No matter where you live or what distance you run/race, distance runners are a friendly crew. We like to wave hello to each other while we're putting in our miles outside. We like to cheer for each other and run together during races. We like to compare race times. We like running on treadmills. We also love to talk about pretty much any running related topic (i.e. the best pre-race meal, what race you're training for, etc.). During a recent conversation with running friends, we developed a list that most runners can relate to. We called our list, **"You might be a runner if..."**

- *You've (ah-hem!) ruined your shorts*
- *You spit*
- *You've read Born to Run and then tried to run barefoot or with Vibram Shoes (and then if you're like me, gotten injured)*
- *You stay in on a Friday night to rest up for your Saturday morning long run*
- *You love Steve Prefontaine*
- *You've been caught squatting (using the bathroom somewhere outside)- usually by a cyclist who creeps up too quickly*
- *You've tried to cover a bodily noise with a cough*
- *You stay up until 2AM to watch the Olympic distance track races on Television (they only seem to play sprints during regular hours)--it's kind of like the Royal Wedding*
- *You get more excited to buy running shoes (or clothes) than, well, most anything else*
- *You've put Vaseline somewhere on your body before a run You pay attention to the color of your urine (aka hydration monitor)*

- *You don't laugh at the word Fartlick (okay, I still laugh. Who came up with that word anyway?)*
- *You love The Eye of the Tiger song and feel like running every time you hear it played*
- *You explain to your spouse or housemates that it's not you that smells, it's just your running clothes*
  You like the taste of Vanilla Bean Gu
- You've prepared an ice bath for yourself, in the winter
- You schedule your dinner dates for later in the evening so you have time to come home from work and run first
- You would rather spend $30 on compression socks than go out for a drink with friends
- Someone asks you how far you jog and you roll your eyes. *Jog? I run.*
- You know what body glide is
- You've ever said... Oh, __ (insert number here) miles? It's just an easy run.
- You've ever been mad at a stop light when you have the walk sign and the stopped car pulled into the crosswalk
- You've ever said... "I'm carb-loading!", "I hit the wall", or "I'll never run a marathon again!"
- You've lost a toenail and instead of thinking it's gross, you celebrate it as a sign of strength
- For the males...if you've have bloody nipples
- For the females...if you've had bloody shorts
- You talk about negative splits
- Bring your running shoes on vacation (who wouldn't?)
- You add the phrase, "I've got a long run in the morning" onto any sentence (i.e. I'm ordering a pizza, I've got a long run in the morning)

If you're new to running- please don't be scared away by the above list! Running is one of the oldest sports around and it's a great sport. One of my favorite things about running is that it reminds each of us, that you can set a goal and with hard work and dedication, you can reach it. You can succeed. You can be anything you want to be. It just takes perseverance and passion.

• • •

It takes you stating your goal and then going after it. You can do this.

Whether you're running to stay healthy and in shape or you're running to achieve a specific time (race) goal, this book is for you. It's time to pick a workout that's right for you and hop on the treadmill for a great workout!

INSTRUCTIONS

TREADMILL TRAINING offers 90 treadmill workouts. Workouts are designed for every level runner; beginning, intermediate and advanced. First, choose the section that is appropriate for you at this time. (NOTE: each section provides base race times for the specific distance it refers to.)

Each workout is based off of your goal (5K, 10K, ½ Marathon, or Marathon) time. To find your specific treadmill workout pace, locate the workout you wish to utilize then access the corresponding pace chart in the back of the book. Looking at your chosen treadmill workout and the appropriate pace chart, write your goal times/paces on a post-it note and tape it to your treadmill for easy reference on your run.

~

Beginner
5K to 10K Workouts

~

Beginner 5K – 10K

Female: training for your first 5k or best time of 28:00+

Male: training for your first 5k or best time of 25:00+

The workouts in this section are designed for first time 5K runners or those with a personal best time of 28 minutes or above for females, and 25 minutes or above for males.

Before each workout it is strongly recommended to do a warm up. After each workout it is highly advisable to perform cool down activities.

Each workout provides sample treadmill running paces based on your 5K goal pace. Additional 5K goal times and respective paces can be found in the charts section (located at the end of this book).

"Every pro was once an amateur, every expert was once a beginner, so dream big and start now."

400 DAY

1st, 2nd, 3rd 400's (.25 Miles) with 30 Second break after each 400

4th, 5th, 6th 400's (.25 Miles) with 60 Second break after each 400

7th, 8th 400's (.25 Miles) with 90 Second break after each 400

Start at Threshold Pace then increase .1 MPH in speed each 400

TOTAL DISTANCE = 2.0 MILES

What you need to know for this workout:
Threshold Pace

Example Female (28:00 5K Goal)

0 - .25 Miles = 6.3 MPH
.25 - .5 Miles = 6.4 MPH
.5 - .75 Miles = 6.5 MPH
.75 – 1.0 Mile = 6.6 MPH
1.0 – 1.25 Miles =6.7 MPH
1.25 – 1.5 Miles = 6.8 MPH
1.5 – 1.75 Miles = 6.9 MPH
1.75 – 2.0 Miles = 7.0 MPH

Example Male (25:00 5K Goal)

0 - .25 Miles = 7.1 MPH
.25 - .5 Miles = 7.2 MPH
.5 - .75 Miles =7.3 MPH
.75 – 1.0 Mile = 7.4 MPH
1.0 – 1.25 Miles = 7.5 MPH
1.25 – 1.5 Miles = 7.6 MPH
1.5 – 1.75 Miles = 7.7 MPH
1.75 – 2.0 Miles = 7.8 MPH

10 Minutes In...

:15 Second run at 5K pace

:45 Second run at Marathon Pace

Repeat 10 times

TOTAL DISTANCE = 1 - 1.25 MILES

What you need to know for this workout:
5k Pace, Marathon Pace

Example Female (28:30 5K Goal)	Example Male (25:30 5K Goal)
0 – :15 Seconds = 6.5 MPH	0 – :15 Seconds = 7.3 MPH
:15 – 1 Minute = 5.8 MPH	:15 – 1 Minute = 6.5 MPH
1:00 – 1:15 Minutes = 6.5 MPH	1:00 – 1:15 Minutes = 7.3 MPH
1:15 – 2:00 Minutes = 5.8 MPH	1:15 – 2:00 Minutes = 6.5 MPH
2:00 – 2:15 Minutes = 6.5 MPH	2:00 – 2:15 Minutes = 7.3 MPH
2:15 – 3:00 Minutes = 5.8 MPH	2:15 – 3:00 Minutes = 6.5 MPH
3:00 – 3:15 Minutes = 6.5 MPH	3:00 – 3:15 Minutes = 7.3 MPH
3:15 – 4:00 Minutes = 5.8 MPH	3:15 – 4:00 Minutes = 6.5 MPH
4:00 – 4:15 Minutes = 6.5 MPH	4:00 – 4:15 Minutes = 7.3 MPH
4:15 – 5:00 Minutes = 5.8 MPH	4:15 – 5:00 Minutes = 6.5 MPH
5:00 – 5:15 Minutes = 6.5 MPH	5:00 – 5:15 Minutes = 7.3 MPH
5:15 – 6:00 Minutes = 5.8 MPH	5:15 – 6:00 Minutes = 6.5 MPH
6:00 – 6:15 Minutes = 6.5 MPH	6:00 – 6:15 Minutes = 7.3 MPH
6:15 – 7:00 Minutes = 5.8 MPH	6:15 – 7:00 Minutes = 6.5 MPH
7:00 – 7:15 Minutes = 6.5 MPH	7:00 – 7:15 Minutes = 7.3 MPH
7:15 – 8:00 Minutes = 5.8 MPH	7:15 – 8:00 Minutes = 6.5 MPH
8:00 – 8:15 Minutes = 6.5 MPH	8:00 – 8:15 Minutes = 7.3 MPH
8:15 – 9:00 Minutes = 5.8 MPH	8:15 – 9:00 Minutes = 6.5 MPH
9:00 – 9:15 Minutes = 6.5 MPH	9:00 – 9:15 Minutes = 7.3 MPH
9:15 – 10:00 Minutes = 5.8 MPH	9:15 – 10:00 Minutes = 6.5MPH

Faster and Faster

1.0 Mile at Threshold Pace

.75 Miles at 10K Pace

.50 Miles at 5K Pace

.25 Miles at Mile pace

No Break Between repetitions

TOTAL DISTANCE = 2.5 MILES

What you need to know for this workout:
Threshold Pace, 10K Pace, 5k Pace, Mile Pace

Example Female (29:00 5K Goal)

0 – 1.0 Mile = 6.1 MPH
1.0 – 1.75 Miles = 6.2 MPH
1.75 – 2.25 Miles = 6.4 MPH
2.25 – 2.5 Miles = 6.9 MPH

Example Male (26:00 5K Goal)

0 – 1.0 Mile = 6.8 MPH
1.0 – 1.75 Miles = 6.9 MPH
1.75 – 2.25 Miles = 7.2 MPH
2.25 – 2.5 Miles = 7.6 MPH

Pace Work

3 Minutes at Marathon Pace

1 Minute at 5K Pace * 6 repetitions

No Break Between Repetitions

TOTAL DISTANCE = 2 - 2.5 MILES

What you need to know for this workout:
Marathon Pace, 5k Pace

Example Female (29:30 5K Goal)	Example Male (26:30 5K Goal)
0 – 3 Minutes = 5.6 MPH	0 – 3 Minutes = 6.3 MPH
3 – 4 Minutes = 6.3 MPH	3 – 4 Minutes = 7.0 MPH
4 – 7 Minutes = 5.6 MPH	4 – 7 Minutes = 6.3 MPH
7 – 8 Minutes = 6.3 MPH	7 – 8 Minutes = 7.0 MPH
8 – 11 Minutes = 5.6 MPH	8 – 11 Minutes = 6.3 MPH
11 – 12 Minutes = 6.3 MPH	11 – 12 Minutes = 7.0 MPH
12 – 15 Minutes = 5.6 MPH	12 – 15 Minutes = 6.3 MPH
15 – 16 Minutes = 6.3 MPH	15 – 16 Minutes = 7.0 MPH
16 – 19 Minutes = 5.6 MPH	16 – 19 Minutes = 6.3 MPH
19 – 20 Minutes = 6.3 MPH	19 – 20 Minutes = 7.0 MPH
20 – 23 Minutes = 5.6 MPH	20 – 23 Minutes = 6.3 MPH
23 – 24 Minutes = 6.3 MPH	23 – 24 Minutes = 7.0 MPH

Pace That 5K

4 * 2 Minutes at 5K Pace rest :60 Seconds between repetitions

3 * 90 Seconds at 5K pace rest :45 Seconds between repetitions

2 * 1 Minute at 5K pace rest :30 Seconds between repetitions

1 * :30 Seconds at 5K pace

TOTAL DISTANCE = 1 - 1.5 MILES

What you need to know for this workout:
5k Pace

Example Female (30:00 5K Goal)	Example Male (27:00 5K Goal)
0 – 2 Minutes = 6.2 MPH	0 – 2 Minutes = 6.9 MPH
2 – 3 Minutes = REST	2 – 3 Minutes = REST
3 – 5 Minutes = 6.2 MPH	3 – 5 Minutes = 6.9 MPH
5 – 6 Minutes = REST	5 – 6 Minutes = REST
6 – 8 Minutes = 6.2 MPH	6 – 8 Minutes = 6.9 MPH
8 – 9 Minutes = REST	8 – 9 Minutes = REST
9 – 11 Minutes = 6.2 MPH	9 – 11 Minutes = 6.9 MPH
11 – 12 Minutes = REST	11 – 12 Minutes = REST
12 – 13:30 Minutes = 6.2 MPH	12 – 13:30 Minutes = 6.9 MPH
13:30 – 14:15 Minutes = REST	13:30 – 14:15 Minutes = REST
14:15 – 15:45 Minutes = 6.2 MPH	14:15 – 15:45 Minutes = 6.9 MPH
15:45 – 16:30 Minutes = REST	15:45 – 16:30 Minutes = REST
16:30 – 18:00 Minutes = 6.2 MPH	16:30 – 18:00 Minutes = 6.9 MPH
18:00 – 18:45 Minutes = REST	18:00 – 18:45 Minutes = REST
18:45 – 19:45 Minutes = 6.2 MPH	18:45 – 19:45 Minutes = 6.9 MPH
19:45 – 20:15 Minutes = REST	19:45 – 20:15 Minutes = REST
20:15 – 21:15 Minutes = 6.2 MPH	20:15 – 21:15 Minutes = 6.9 MPH
21:15 – 21:45 Minutes = REST	21:15 – 21:45 Minutes = REST
21:45 – 22:15 Minutes = 6.2 MPH	21:45 – 22:15 Minutes = 6.9 MPH

Switching Gears

1 Minute @ 10k Pace

:50 Seconds @ 5K pace

:40 Seconds @ 1600 pace

:30 Seconds @ 800 Pace

:20 Seconds @ 400 pace

Repeat Sequence 2 additional times

Rest 30 Seconds between repetitions and 2 Minutes after each sequence

TOTAL DISTANCE = 1 - 1.25 Miles

What you need to know for this workout:
10K Pace, 5K Pace, 1600 Pace, 800 Pace, 400 Pace

Example Female (31:00 5K Goal)	Example Male (27:30 5K Goal)
0 – 1 Minute = 5.9 MPH	0 – 1 Minute = 6.5 MPH
1 – 1:30 Minutes = REST	1 – 1:30 Minutes = REST
1:30 – 2:20 Minutes = 6.0 MPH	1:30 – 2:20 Minutes = 6.8 MPH
2:20 – 2:50 Minutes = REST	2:20 – 2:50 Minutes = REST
2:50 – 3:30 Minutes = 6.4 MPH	2:50 – 3:30 Minutes = 7.2 MPH
3:30 – 4:00 Minutes = REST	3:30 – 4:00 Minutes = REST
4:00 – 4:30 Minutes = 6.6 MPH	4:00 – 4:30 Minutes = 7.4 MPH
4:30 – 5:00 Minutes = REST	4:30 – 5:00 Minutes = REST
5:00 – 5:20 Minutes = 6.9 MPH	5:00 – 5:20 Minutes = 7.7 MPH
Rest 2 Minutes and Repeat	Rest 2 Minutes and Repeat
Sequence 2 Times	Sequence 2 Times

<u>Meet Me Halfway</u>

Start at Marathon Pace for 1 Minute

Next Minute increase to 400 pace

Continue to increase from Marathon Pace by .1 MPH each odd minute

Decrease from 400 pace .1 MPH each even minute until you meet in the middle of the pace.

TOTAL DISTANCE = 1.75 - 2.25 MILES

What you need to know for this workout:
400 Pace, Marathon Pace

<u>Example Female (32:00 5K Goal)</u>	<u>Example Male (28:00 5K Goal)</u>
0 – 1 Minute = 5.2 MPH	0 – 1 Minute = 5.9 MPH
1 – 2 Minutes = 6.7 MPH	1 – 2 Minutes = 7.5 MPH
2 – 3 Minutes = 5.3 MPH	2 – 3 Minutes = 6.0 MPH
3 – 4 Minutes = 6.6 MPH	3 – 4 Minutes = 7.4 MPH
4 – 5 Minutes = 5.4 MPH	4 – 5 Minutes = 6.1 MPH
5 – 6 Minutes = 6.5 MPH	5 – 6 Minutes = 7.3 MPH
6 – 7 Minutes = 5.5 MPH	6 – 7 Minutes = 6.2 MPH
7 – 8 Minutes = 6.4 MPH	7 – 8 Minutes = 7.2 MPH
8 – 9 Minutes = 5.6 MPH	8 – 9 Minutes = 6.3 MPH
9 – 10 Minutes = 6.3 MPH	9 – 10 Minutes = 7.1 MPH
10 – 11 Minutes = 5.7 MPH	10 – 11 Minutes = 6.4 MPH
11 – 12 Minutes = 6.2 MPH	11 – 12 Minutes = 7.0 MPH
12 – 13 Minutes = 5.8 MPH	12 – 13 Minutes = 6.5 MPH
13 – 14 Minutes = 6.1 MPH	13 – 14 Minutes = 6.9 MPH
14 – 15 Minutes = 5.9 MPH	14 – 15 Minutes = 6.6 MPH
15 – 16 Minutes = 6.0 MPH	15 – 16 Minutes = 6.8 MPH
	16 – 17 Minutes = 6.7 MPH

Up and Back Down

1 Minute at 5K pace

1 Minute at Marathon Pace

3 Minutes at 5k pace

3 Minutes at Marathon Pace

5 Minutes at 5K pace

5 Minutes at Marathon Pace

3 Minutes at 5K pace

3 Minutes at Marathon pace

1 Minute at 5K pace

1 Minute at Marathon Pace

TOTAL DISTANCE = 1.75 - 2.25 MILES

What you need to know for this workout:
5K Pace, Marathon Pace

Example Female (33:00 5K Goal)	Example Male (28:30 5K Goal)
0 – 1 Minute = 5.6 MPH	0 – 1 Minute = 6.5 MPH
1 – 2 Minutes = 5.1 MPH	1 – 2 Minutes = 5.8 MPH
2 – 5 Minutes = 5.6 MPH	2 – 5 Minutes = 6.5 MPH
5 – 8 Minutes = 5.1 MPH	5 – 8 Minutes = 5.8 MPH
8 – 13 Minutes = 5.6 MPH	8 – 13 Minutes = 6.5 MPH
13 – 18 Minutes = 5.1 MPH	13 – 18 Minutes = 5.8 MPH
18 – 21 Minutes = 5.6 MPH	18 – 21 Minutes = 6.5 MPH
21 – 24 Minutes = 5.1 MPH	21 – 24 Minutes = 5.8 MPH
25 – 25 Minutes = 5.6 MPH	24 – 25 Minutes = 6.5 MPH
25 – 26 Minutes = 5.1 MPH	25 – 26 Minutes = 5.8 MPH

4 Mile Session

1 Mile at Marathon Pace

1 Mile at Threshold Pace

1 Mile at 10K Pace

1 Mile at 5K Pace

Rest 5 Minutes after each mile

TOTAL DISTANCE = 4 MILES

What you need to know for this workout:
Marathon Pace, Threshold Pace, 10K Pace, 5K Pace

Example Female (34:00 5K Goal)	Example Male (29:00 5K Goal)
0 – 1 Mile = 4.9 MPH	0 – 1 Mile = 5.7 MPH
REST 5 MINUTES	REST 5 MINUTES
1 – 2 Miles = 5.2 MPH	1 – 2 Miles = 6.1 MPH
REST 5 MINUTES	REST 5 MINUTES
2 – 3 Miles = 5.3 MPH	2 – 3 Miles = 6.2 MPH
REST 5 MINUTES	REST 5 MINUTES
3 – 4 Miles = 5.5 MPH	3 – 4 Miles = 6.4 MPH

<u>2 to 1</u>

2 Minutes at 5K pace

1 Minute at Marathon Pace

Repeat 10 Times – No Rest between repetitions

TOTAL DISTANCE = 2.25 - 3.0 MILES

What you need to know for this workout:
Marathon Pace, 5K Pace

Example Female (35:00 5K Goal)	Example Male (29:30 5K Goal)
0 – 2 Minutes = 5.3 MPH	0 – 2 Minutes = 6.3 MPH
2 – 3 Minutes = 4.8 MPH	2 – 3 Minutes = 5.6 MPH
3 – 5 Minutes = 5.3 MPH	3 – 5 Minutes = 6.3 MPH
5 – 6 Minutes = 4.8 MPH	5 – 6 Minutes = 5.6 MPH
6 – 8 Minutes = 5.3 MPH	6 – 8 Minutes = 6.3 MPH
8 – 9 Minutes = 4.8 MPH	8 – 9 Minutes = 5.6 MPH
9 – 11 Minutes = 5.3 MPH	9 – 11 Minutes = 6.3 MPH
11 – 12 Minutes = 4.8 MPH	11 – 12 Minutes = 5.6 MPH
12 – 14 Minutes = 5.3 MPH	12 – 14 Minutes = 6.3 MPH
14 – 15 Minutes = 4.8 MPH	14 – 15 Minutes = 5.6 MPH
15 – 17 Minutes = 5.3 MPH	15 – 17 Minutes = 6.3 MPH
17 – 18 Minutes = 4.8 MPH	17 – 18 Minutes = 5.6 MPH
18 – 20 Minutes = 5.3 MPH	18 – 20 Minutes = 6.3 MPH
20 – 21 Minutes = 4.8 MPH	20 – 21 Minutes = 5.6 MPH
21 – 23 Minutes = 5.3 MPH	21 – 23 Minutes = 6.3 MPH
23 – 24 Minutes = 4.8 MPH	23 – 24 Minutes = 5.6 MPH
24 – 26 Minutes = 5.3 MPH	24 – 26 Minutes = 6.3 MPH
26 – 27 Minutes = 4.8 MPH	26 – 27 Minutes = 5.6 MPH
27 – 29 Minutes = 5.3 MPH	27 – 29 Minutes = 6.3 MPH
29 – 30 Minutes = 4.8 MPH	29 – 30 Minutes = 5.6 MPH

~
Beginner
½ Marathon Workouts
~

Beginner ½ Marathon

Female: training for your first ½ Marathon or best time of 2:00 hours +

Male: training for your first ½ Marathon or best time of 1:45 +

The workouts in this section are designed for first time ½ Marathon runners or those with a personal best time of 2 hours or above for females, and 1 hour and 45 minutes or above for males.

Before each workout it is strongly recommended to do a warm up. After each workout it is highly advisable to perform cool down activities.

Each workout provides sample treadmill running paces based on your ½ Marathon goal pace. Additional ½ Marathon goal times and respective paces can be found in the charts section (located at the end of this book).

"You have a choice: you can throw in the towel or you can use it to wipe the sweat from your face."

10's

10 Minutes at Marathon Pace

10 Minutes at Half Marathon Pace

10 Minutes at Marathon Pace

10 Minutes at Half Marathon Pace

TOTAL DISTANCE =   4.5 - 5.5 MILES

What you need to know for this workout:
Marathon Pace, Half Marathon Pace

Example Female (2:00 13.1 Goal)

0 – 10 Minutes = 6.4 MPH
10 – 20 Minutes = 6.6 MPH
20 – 30 Minutes = 6.4 MPH
30 – 40 Minutes = 6.6 MPH

Example Male (1:45 13.1 Goal)

0 – 10 Minutes = 7.2 MPH
10 – 20 Minutes = 7.5 MPH
20 – 30 Minutes = 7.2 MPH
30 – 40 Minutes = 7.5 MPH

Change is a Given

1 Minute at 5k Pace

2 Minutes at 10K Pace

3 Minutes at Threshold Pace

4 Minutes at Half Marathon Pace

5 Minutes at Marathon Pace

Repeat Sequence

Rest 3-5 Minutes between each sequence

TOTAL DISTANCE =   3.0 - 3.75 MILES

What you need to know for this workout:
Marathon Pace, Half Marathon Pace, Threshold Pace, 10K Pace,
5K Pace

Example Female (2:10 13.1 Goal)	Example Male (1:50 13.1 Goal)
0 – 1 Minute = 6.6 MPH	0 – 1 Minute = 7.8 MPH
1 – 3 Minutes = 6.4 MPH	1 – 3 Minutes = 7.5 MPH
3 – 6 Minutes = 6.3 MPH	3 – 6 Minutes = 7.4 MPH
6 – 10 Minutes =6.1 MPH	6 – 10 Minutes =7.2 MPH
10 – 15 Minutes = 5.9 MPH	10 – 15 Minutes = 6.9 MPH
Rest 3 -5 Minutes	Rest 3 – 5 Minutes
Repeat	Repeat

120 On / 60 Off

120 Seconds at Half Marathon Pace

60 Seconds at Marathon Pace

Repeat 9 Times (total of 10 sequences)

TOTAL DISTANCE =   2.75 - 3.75 MILES

What you need to know for this workout:
Marathon Pace, Half Marathon Pace

Example Female (2:20 13.1 Goal)	Example Male (1:55 13.1 Goal)
0 – 2 Minutes = 5.6 MPH	0 – 2 Minutes = 6.8 MPH
2 – 3 Minutes = 5.5 MPH	2 – 3 Minutes = 6.6 MPH
3 – 5 Minutes = 5.6 MPH	3 – 5 Minutes = 6.8 MPH
5 – 6 Minutes = 5.5 MPH	5 – 6 Minutes = 6.6 MPH
6 – 8 Minutes = 5.6 MPH	6 – 8 Minutes = 6.8 MPH
8 – 9 Minutes = 5.5 MPH	8 – 9 Minutes = 6.6 MPH
9 – 11 Minutes = 5.6 MPH	9 – 11 Minutes = 6.8 MPH
11 – 12 Minutes = 5.5 MPH	11 – 12 Minutes = 6.6 MPH
12 – 14 Minutes = 5.6 MPH	12 – 14 Minutes = 6.8 MPH
14 – 15 Minutes = 5.5 MPH	14 – 15 Minutes = 6.6 MPH
15 – 17 Minutes = 5.6 MPH	15 – 17 Minutes = 6.8 MPH
17 – 18 Minutes = 5.5 MPH	17 – 18 Minutes = 6.6 MPH
18 – 20 Minutes = 5.6 MPH	18 – 20 Minutes = 6.8 MPH
20 – 21 Minutes = 5.5 MPH	20 – 21 Minutes = 6.6 MPH
21 – 23 Minutes = 5.6 MPH	21 – 23 Minutes = 6.8 MPH
23 – 24 Minutes = 5.5 MPH	23 – 24 Minutes = 6.6 MPH
24 – 26 Minutes = 5.6 MPH	24 – 26 Minutes = 6.8 MPH
26 – 27 Minutes = 5.5 MPH	26 – 27 Minutes = 6.6 MPH
27 – 29 Minutes = 5.6 MPH	27 – 29 Minutes = 6.8 MPH
29 – 30 Minutes = 5.5 MPH	29 – 30 Minutes = 6.6 MPH

<u>Tempo Training</u>

15 Minutes at Threshold Pace

15 Minutes at .5 MPH slower than Marathon Pace

15 Minutes at Threshold Pace

15 Minutes at .5 MPH slower than Marathon Pace

TOTAL DISTANCE =   5.0 - 6.5 MILES

What you need to know for this workout:
Marathon Pace, Threshold Pace

Example Female (2:30 13.1 Goal)	Example Male (2:00 13.1 Goal)
0 – 15 Minutes = 5.5 MPH	0 – 15 Minutes = 6.8 MPH
15 – 30 Minutes = 4.7 MPH	15 – 30 Minutes = 5.9 MPH
30 – 45 Minutes = 5.5 MPH	30 – 45 Minutes = 6.8 MPH
45 – 60 Minutes = 4.7 MPH	45 – 60 Minutes = 5.9 MPH

Race Simulation

5 Minutes at .5 MPH Slower than Marathon Pace

20 Minutes at Marathon Pace

20 Minutes at Half Marathon Pace

5 Minutes at 10K pace

60 Seconds at 5k Pace

TOTAL DISTANCE =   5 - 6.5 MILES

What you need to know for this workout:
Marathon Pace, Half Marathon Pace, 10K Pace, 5K Pace

Example Female (2:00 13.1 Goal)	Example Male (1:45 13.1 Goal)
0 – 5 Minutes = 5.9 MPH	0 – 5 Minutes = 6.7 MPH
5 – 25 Minutes = 6.4 MPH	5 – 25 Minutes = 7.2 MPH
25 – 45 Minutes = 6.6 MPH	25 – 45 Minutes = 7.5 MPH
45 – 50 Minutes = 6.9 MPH	45 – 50 Minutes = 7.9 MPH
50 – 51 Minutes = 7.2 MPH	50 – 51 Minutes = 8.1 MPH

316293

3 Minutes at Marathon Pace

1 Minute at 10K pace

6 Minutes at Marathon Pace

2 Minutes at 10K pace

9 Minutes at Marathon Pace

3 Minutes at 10K Pace

Rest 3-5 Minutes between Sequences

Repeat Sequence

TOTAL DISTANCE = 4.75 - 6.0 MILES

What you need to know for this workout:
Marathon Pace, 10K Pace

Example Female (2:10 13.1 Goal)	Example Male (1:50 13.1 Goal)
0 – 3 Minutes = 5.9 MPH	0 – 3 Minutes = 6.9 MPH
3 – 4 Minutes = 6.4 MPH	3 – 4 Minutes = 7.5 MPH
4 – 10 Minutes = 5.9 MPH	4 – 10 Minutes = 6.9 MPH
10 – 12 Minutes = 6.4 MPH	10 – 12 Minutes = 7.5 MPH
12 – 21 Minutes = 5.9 MPH	12 – 21 Minutes = 6.9 MPH
21 – 24 Minutes = 6.4 MPH	21 – 24 Minutes = 7.5 MPH
Rest 3 – 5 Minutes	Rest 3 – 5 Minutes
Repeat	Repeat

Hilly Terrain

Set Incline to 2%

2 Miles at Marathon Pace

Set Incline to 3%

1 Mile at Marathon Pace

Set Incline to 4%

.5 Miles at .5 MPH Slower than Marathon Pace

Rest 3-5 Minutes between sequences

Repeat Sequence

TOTAL DISTANCE = 7 MILES

What you need to know for this workout:
Marathon Pace

Example Female (2:20 13.1 Goal)	Example Male (1:55 13.1 Goal)
0 – 2 Miles = 5.5 MPH @ 2% Incline	0 – 2 Miles = 6.6 MPH @ 2% Incline
2 – 3 Miles = 5.5 MPH @ 3% Incline	2 – 3 Miles = 6.6 MPH @ 3% Incline
3 – 3.5 Miles = 5.0 MPH @ 4% Incline	3 – 3.5 Miles = 6.1 MPH @ 4%Incline
Rest 3 – 5 Minutes	Rest 3 – 5 Minutes
Repeat	Repeat

Can You Do This?

1 Mile at Marathon Pace

4 Miles at Half Marathon Pace

1 Mile at Marathon Pace

TOTAL DISTANCE = 6 MILES

What you need to know for this workout:
Marathon Pace, Half Marathon Pace

Example Female (2:30 13.1 Goal)

0 – 1 Mile = 5.2 MPH
1 – 5 Miles = 5.3 MPH
5 – 6 Miles = 5.2 MPH

Example Male (2:00 13.1 Goal)

0 – 1 Mile = 6.4 MPH
1 – 5 Miles = 6.6 MPH
5 – 6 Miles = 6.4 MPH

Get The Distance Done

1 Mile at .5 MPH Slower than Marathon Pace

1 Mile at Marathon Pace

1 Mile at Half Marathon Pace

1 Mile at .5 MPH Slower than Marathon Pace

1 Mile at Marathon Pace

1 Mile at Half Marathon Pace

1 Mile at .5 MPH Slower than Marathon Pace

1 Mile at Marathon Pace

1 Mile at Half Marathon Pace

1 Mile at .5 MPH Slower than Marathon Pace

1 Mile at Marathon Pace

1 Mile at Half Marathon Pace

1 Mile at Marathon Pace

.1 Mile at 10K Pace

TOTAL DISTANCE =   13.1 MILES

What you need to know for this workout:
Marathon Pace, Half Marathon Pace, 10K Pace

Example Female (2:00 13.1 Goal)

0 – 1 Mile = 5.9 MPH
1 – 2 Miles = 6.4 MPH
2 – 3 Miles = 6.6 MPH
3 – 4 Miles = 5.9 MPH
4 – 5 Miles = 6.4 MPH
5 – 6 Miles = 6.6 MPH
6 – 7 Miles = 5.9 MPH
7 – 8 Miles = 6.4 MPH
8 – 9 Miles =6.6 MPH
9 – 10 Miles = 5.9 MPH
10 – 11 Miles = 6.4 MPH
11 – 12 Miles = 6.6 MPH
12 – 13 Miles = 6.4 MPH
13 – 13.1 Miles = 6.9 MPH

Example Male (1:45 13.1 Goal)

0 – 1 Mile = 6.7 MPH
1 – 2 Miles = 7.2 MPH
2 – 3 Miles = 7.5 MPH
3 - 4 Miles = 6.7 MPH
4 – 5 Miles = 7.2 MPH
5 – 6 Miles = 7.5 MPH
6 – 7 Miles = 6.7 MPH
7 – 8 Miles = 7.2 MPH
8 – 9 Miles =7.5 MPH
9 – 10 Miles = 6.7 MPH
10 – 11 Miles = 7.2 MPH
11 – 12 Miles = 7.5 MPH
12 – 13 Miles = 7.2 MPH
13 – 13.1 Miles = 7.9 MPH

800 / 400

800 at Half Marathon Pace

400 at Marathon Pace

Repeat 9 Times (total of 10 sequences)

TOTAL DISTANCE = 7.5 MILES

What you need to know for this workout:
Marathon Pace, Half Marathon Pace

Example Female (2:10 13.1 Goal)	Example Male (1:50 13.1 Goal)
0 – .5 Miles = 6.1 MPH	0 - .5 Miles = 7.2 MPH
.5 – .75 Miles = 5.9 MPH	.5 - .75 Miles = 6.9 MPH
.75 – 1.25 Miles = 6.1 MPH	.75 – 1.25 Miles = 7.2 MPH
1.25 – 1.5 Miles = 5.9 MPH	1.25 – 1.5 Miles = 6.9 MPH
1.5 – 2.0 Miles = 6.1 MPH	1.5 – 2.0 Miles = 7.2 MPH
2.0 – 2.25 Miles = 5.9 MPH	2.0 – 2.25 Miles = 6.9 MPH
2.25 – 2.75 Miles = 6.1 MPH	2.25 – 2.75 Miles = 7.2 MPH
2.75 – 3.0 Miles = 5.9 MPH	2.75 – 3.0 Miles = 6.9 MPH
3.0 – 3.5 Miles = 6.1 MPH	3.0 – 3.5 Miles = 7.2 MPH
3.5 – 3.75 Miles = 5.9 MPH	3.5 – 3.75 Miles = 6.9 MPH
3.75 – 4.25 Miles = 6.1 MPH	3.75 – 4.25 Miles = 7.2 MPH
4.25 – 4.5 Miles = 5.9 MPH	4.25 – 4.5 Miles = 6.9 MPH
4.5 – 5.0 Miles = 6.1 MPH	4.5 – 5.0 Miles = 7.2 MPH
5.0 – 5.25 Miles = 5.9 MPH	5.0 – 5.25 Miles = 6.9 MPH
5.25 – 5.75 Miles = 6.1 MPH	5.25 – 5.75 Miles = 7.2 MPH
5.75 – 6.0 Miles = 5.9 MPH	5.75 – 6.0 Miles = 6.9 MPH
6.0 – 6.5 Miles = 6.1 MPH	6.0 – 6.5 Miles = 7.2 MPH
6.5 – 6.75 Miles = 5.9 MPH	6.5 – 6.75 Miles = 6.9 MPH
6.75 – 7.25 Miles = 6.1 MPH	6.75 – 7.25 Miles = 7.2 MPH
7.25 – 7.5 Miles = 5.9 MPH	7.25 – 7.5 Miles = 6.9 MPH

~

Beginner
Marathon Workouts

~

Beginner Marathon

Female: training for your first Marathon or best time of 4:00 hours +

Male: training for your first Marathon or best time of 3:30+

The workouts in this section are designed for first time Marathon runners or those with a personal best time of 4 hours or above for females, and 3 hours and 30 minutes or above for males.

Before each workout it is strongly recommended to do a warm up. After each workout it is highly advisable to perform cool down activities.

Each workout provides sample treadmill running paces based on your Marathon goal pace. Additional Marathon goal times and respective paces can be found in the charts section (located at the end of this book).

"At Mile 20 I thought I was dead, At mile 22 I wished I was dead, At Mile 24 I knew I was dead, At mile 26.2, I know I had become too tough to kill."

Mile High Club

1 Mile at 60% Marathon Pace

1 Mile at 65% Marathon Pace

1 Mile at 70% Marathon Pace

1 Mile at 75% Marathon Pace

1 Mile at 80% Marathon Pace

1 Mile at 85% Marathon Pace

1 Mile at 90% Marathon Pace

TOTAL DISTANCE = 7 MILES

What you need to know for this workout:
60% Marathon Pace, 65% Marathon Pace, 70% Marathon Pace,
75% Marathon Pace, 80% Marathon Pace, 85% Marathon Pace,
90% Marathon Pace

Example Female (4:00 26.2 Goal)	Example Male (3:30 26.2 Goal)
0 – 1 Mile = 4.7 MPH	0 – 1 Mile = 5.3 MPH
1 – 2 Miles = 4.9 MPH	1 – 2 Miles = 5.6 MPH
2 – 3 Miles = 5.0 MPH	2 – 3 Miles = 5.8 MPH
3 – 4 Miles = 5.2 MPH	3 – 4 Miles = 6.0 MPH
4 – 5 Miles = 5.5 MPH	4 – 5 Miles = 6.2 MPH
5 – 6 Miles = 5.7 MPH	5 – 6 Miles = 6.5 MPH
6 – 7 Miles = 6.0 MPH	6 – 7 Miles = 6.8 MPH

Run For The Hills

.5 Miles at 60% Marathon Pace, incline 0%

.5 Miles at 60% Marathon Pace, incline 1%

.5 Miles at 60% Marathon Pace, incline 2%

.5 Miles at 60% Marathon Pace, incline 3%

.5 Miles at 60% Marathon Pace, incline 4%

Repeat Sequence

TOTAL DISTANCE =   5 MILES

What you need to know for this workout:
60% Marathon Pace

Example Female (4:10 26.2 Goal)	Example Male (3:35 26.2 Goal)
0 - .5 Miles = 4.5 MPH @ 0% Incline	0 - .5 Miles = 5.2 MPH @ 0% Incline
.5 – 1 Mile = 4.5 MPH @ 1% Incline	.5 – 1 Mile = 5.2 MPH @ 1% Incline
1 – 1.5 Miles = 4.5 MPH @ 2% Incline	1 – 1.5 Miles = 5.2 MPH @ 2% Incline
1.5 – 2 Miles = 4.5 MPH @ 3% Incline	1.5 – 2 Miles = 5.2 MPH @ 3% Incline
2 – 2.5 Miles = 4.5 MPH @ 4% Incline	2 – 2.5 Miles = 5.2 MPH @ 4% Incline
Repeat	Repeat

Hit That Pace

10 Minutes at 60% Marathon Pace

1 Minute at 100% Marathon Pace

9 Minutes at 65% Marathon Pace

2 Minutes at 100% Marathon Pace

8 Minutes at 70% Marathon Pace

3 Minutes at 100% Marathon Pace

7 Minutes at 75% Marathon Pace

4 Minutes at 100% Marathon Pace

6 Minutes at 80% Marathon Pace

5 Minutes at 100% Marathon Pace

TOTAL DISTANCE = 5 - 6.5 MILES

What you need to know for this workout:
60% Marathon Pace, 65% Marathon Pace, 70% Marathon Pace,
75% Marathon Pace, 80% Marathon Pace, 100% Marathon Pace

Example Female (4:20 26.2 Goal)	Example Male (3:40 26.2 Goal)
0 – 10 Minutes = 4.3 MPH	0 – 10 Minutes = 5.1 MPH
10 – 11 Minutes = 6.1 MPH	10 – 11 Minutes = 7.1 MPH
11 – 20 Minutes = 4.5 MPH	11 – 20 Minutes = 5.3 MPH
20 – 22 Minutes = 6.1 MPH	20 – 22 Minutes = 7.1 MPH
22 – 30 Minutes = 4.7 MPH	22 – 30 Minutes = 5.5 MPH
30 – 33 Minutes = 6.1 MPH	30 – 33 Minutes = 7.1 MPH
33 – 40 Minutes = 4.8 MPH	33 – 40 Minutes = 5.7 MPH
40 – 44 Minutes = 6.1 MPH	40 – 44 Minutes = 7.1 MPH
44 – 50 Minutes = 5.0 MPH	44 – 50 Minutes = 6.0 MPH
50 – 55 Minutes = 6.1 MPH	50 – 55 Minutes = 7.1 MPH

<u>Race Ready</u>

20 Minutes at 70% Marathon Pace

20 Minutes at 90% Marathon Pace

20 Minutes at 70% Marathon Pace

20 Minutes at 95% Marathon Pace

5 Minutes at 70% Marathon Pace

5 Minutes at 100% Marathon Pace

TOTAL DISTANCE = 7.5 - 9 MILES

What you need to know for this workout:
70% Marathon Pace, 90% Marathon Pace, 95% Marathon Pace,
100% Marathon Pace

<u>Example Female (4:40 26.2 Goal)</u>	<u>Example Male (3:50 26.2 Goal)</u>
0 – 20 Minutes = 4.3 MPH	0 – 20 Minutes = 5.3 MPH
20 – 40 Minutes = 5.1 MPH	20 – 40 Minutes = 6.2 MPH
40 – 60 Minutes = 4.3 MPH	40 – 60 Minutes = 5.3 MPH
60 – 80 Minutes = 5.4 MPH	60 – 80 Minutes = 6.5 MPH
80 – 85 Minutes = 4.3 MPH	80 – 85 Minutes = 5.3 MPH
85 – 90 Minutes = 5.6 MPH	85 – 90 Minutes = 6.8 MPH

Halfway Workout

Start at 60% Marathon Pace

Increase .1 MPH every 800 Meters (.5 miles) until you reach 100% Marathon Pace

Hold 100% Marathon Pace for the remainder of the 13.1 mile run

TOTAL DISTANCE = 13.1 MILES

What you need to know for this workout:
60% Marathon Pace, 100% Marathon Pace

Example Female (5:00 26.2 Goal)	Example Male (4:00 26.2 Goal)
0 - .5 Miles = 3.7 MPH	0 - .5 Miles = 4.7 MPH
.5 – 1.0 Miles = 3.8 MPH	.5 – 1.0 Miles = 4.8 MPH
1.0 – 1.5 Miles = 3.9 MPH	1.0 – 1.5 Miles = 4.9 MPH
1.5 – 2.0 Miles = 4.0 MPH	1.5 – 2.0 Miles = 5.0 MPH
2.0 – 2.5 Miles = 4.1 MPH	2.0 – 2.5 Miles = 5.1 MPH
2.5 – 3.0 Miles = 4.2 MPH	2.5 – 3.0 Miles = 5.2 MPH
3.0 – 3.5 Miles =4.3 MPH	3.0 – 3.5 Miles =5.3 MPH
3.5 – 4.0 Miles = 4.4 MPH	3.5 – 4.0 Miles = 5.4 MPH
4.0 – 4.5 Miles = 4.5 MPH	4.0 – 4.5 Miles = 5.5 MPH
4.5 – 5.0 Miles = 4.6 MPH	4.5 – 5.0 Miles = 5.6 MPH
5.0 – 5.5 Miles = 4.7 MPH	5.0 – 5.5 Miles = 5.7 MPH
5.5 – 6.0 Miles = 4.8 MPH	5.5 – 6.0 Miles = 5.8 MPH
6.0 – 6.5 Miles = 4.9 MPH	6.0 – 6.5 Miles = 5.9 MPH
6.5 – 7.0 Miles = 5.0 MPH	6.5 – 7.0 Miles = 6.0 MPH
7.0 – 7.5 Miles = 5.1 MPH	7.0 – 7.5 Miles = 6.1 MPH
7.5 – 8.0 Miles = 5.2 MPH	7.5 – 8.0 Miles = 6.2 MPH
8.0 – 13.1 Miles = 5.3 MPH	8.0 – 8.5 Miles = 6.3 MPH
	8.5 – 9.0 Miles = 6.4 MPH
	9.0 – 9.5 Miles = 6.5 MPH
	9.5 – 13.1 Miles = 6.6 MPH

To The Top and Back

5 Minutes at 60% Marathon Pace

5 Minutes at 65% Marathon Pace

5 Minutes at 70% Marathon Pace

5 Minutes at 75% Marathon Pace

5 Minutes at 80% Marathon Pace

5 Minutes at 85% Marathon Pace

5 Minutes at 90% Marathon Pace

5 Minutes at 95% Marathon Pace

5 Minutes at 100% Marathon Pace

5 Minutes at 90% Marathon Pace

5 Minutes at 80% Marathon Pace

5 Minutes at 70% Marathon Pace

5 Minutes at 60% Marathon Pace

TOTAL DISTANCE =   5 - 7 MILES

What you need to know for this workout:
60% Marathon Pace, 65% Marathon Pace, 70% Marathon Pace,
75% Marathon Pace, 80% Marathon Pace, 85% Marathon Pace,
90% Marathon Pace, 95% Marathon Pace, 100% Marathon Pace

Example Female (4:30 26.2 Goal)

0 – 5 Minutes = 4.2 MPH
5 – 10 Minutes = 4.3 MPH
10 – 15 Minutes =4.5 MPH
15 – 20 Minutes = 4.7 MPH
20 – 25 Minutes = 4.9 MPH
25 – 30 Minutes = 5.1 MPH
30 – 35 Minutes = 5.3 MPH
35 – 40 Minutes = 5.5 MPH
40 – 45 Minutes = 5.8 MPH
45 – 50 Minutes = 5.3 MPH
50 – 55 Minutes = 4.9 MPH
55 – 60 Minutes = 4.5 MPH
60 – 65 Minutes = 4.2 MPH

Example Male (3:45 26.2 Goal)

0 – 5 Minutes = 5.0 MPH
5 – 10 Minutes = 5.2 MPH
10 – 15 Minutes =5.4 MPH
15 – 20 Minutes = 5.6 MPH
20 – 25 Minutes = 5.8 MPH
25 – 30 Minutes = 6.1 MPH
30 – 35 Minutes = 6.4 MPH
35 – 40 Minutes = 6.7 MPH
40 – 45 Minutes = 7.0 MPH
45 – 50 Minutes = 6.4 MPH
50 – 55 Minutes = 5.8 MPH
55 – 60 Minutes = 5.4 MPH
60 – 65 Minutes = 5.0 MPH

Again and Again and Again

1 Minute at 60% Marathon Pace

1 Minute at 90% Marathon Pace

2 Minutes at 60% Marathon Pace

2 Minutes at 90% Marathon Pace

3 Minutes at 60% Marathon Pace

3 Minutes at 90% Marathon Pace

4 Minutes at 60% Marathon Pace

4 Minutes at 90% Marathon Pace

5 Minutes at 60% Marathon Pace

5 Minutes at 90% Marathon Pace

6 Minutes at 60% Marathon Pace

6 Minutes at 90% Marathon Pace

7 Minutes at 60% Marathon Pace

7 Minutes at 90% Marathon Pace

8 Minutes at 60% Marathon Pace

8 Minutes at 90% Marathon Pace

9 Minutes at 60% Marathon Pace

9 Minutes at 90% Marathon Pace

10 Minutes at 60% Marathon Pace

10 Minutes at 90% Marathon Pace

TOTAL DISTANCE = 9 – 11 MILES

What you need to know for this workout:
60% Marathon Pace, 90% Marathon Pace

Example Female (4:50 26.2 Goal)	Example Male (3:55 26.2 Goal)
0 – 1 Minute = 3.9 MPH	0 – 1 Minute = 4.8 MPH
1 – 2 Minutes = 4.9 MPH	1 – 2 Minutes = 6.1 MPH
2 – 4 Minutes = 3.9 MPH	2 – 4 Minutes = 4.8 MPH
4 – 6 Minutes = 4.9 MPH	4 – 6 Minutes = 6.1 MPH
6 – 9 Minutes = 3.9 MPH	6 – 9 Minutes = 4.8 MPH
9 – 12 Minutes = 4.9 MPH	9 – 12 Minutes = 6.1 MPH
12 – 16 Minutes = 3.9 MPH	12 – 16 Minutes = 4.8 MPH
16 – 20 Minutes = 4.9 MPH	16 – 20 Minutes = 6.1 MPH
20 – 25 Minutes = 3.9 MPH	20 – 25 Minutes = 4.8 MPH
25 – 30 Minutes = 4.9 MPH	25 – 30 Minutes = 6.1 MPH
30 – 36 Minutes = 3.9 MPH	30 – 36 Minutes = 4.8 MPH
36 – 42 Minutes = 4.9 MPH	36 – 42 Minutes = 6.1 MPH
42 – 49 Minutes = 3.9 MPH	42 – 49 Minutes = 4.8 MPH
49 – 56 Minutes = 4.9 MPH	49 – 56 Minutes = 6.1 MPH
56 – 64 Minutes = 3.9 MPH	56 – 64 Minutes = 4.8 MPH
64 – 72 Minutes = 4.9 MPH	64 – 72 Minutes = 6.1 MPH
72 – 81 Minutes = 3.9 MPH	72 – 81 Minutes = 4.8 MPH
81 – 90 Minutes = 4.9 MPH	81 – 90 Minutes = 6.1 MPH
90 – 100 Minutes = 3.9 MPH	90 – 100 Minutes = 4.8 MPH
100 – 110 Minutes = 4.9 MPH	100 – 110 Minutes = 6.1 MPH

Lots of 4's

4 Minutes at 60% Marathon Pace

4 Minutes at 80% Marathon Pace

4 Minutes at 60% Marathon Pace

4 Minutes at 85% Marathon Pace

4 Minutes at 60% Marathon Pace

4 Minutes at 90% Marathon Pace

4 Minutes at 60% Marathon Pace

4 Minutes at 95% Marathon Pace

4 Minutes at 60% Marathon Pace

4 Minutes at 100% Marathon Pace

4 Minutes at 60% Marathon Pace

4 Minutes at 105% Marathon Pace

4 Minutes at 60% Marathon Pace

4 Minutes at 110% Marathon Pace

TOTAL DISTANCE = 5 - 7 MILES

What you need to know for this workout:
60% Marathon Pace, 80% Marathon Pace, 85% Marathon Pace,
90% Marathon Pace, 95% Marathon Pace, 100% Marathon Pace,
105% Marathon Pace, 110% Marathon Pace

Example Female (4:20 26.2 Goal)

0 – 4 Minutes = 4.3 MPH
4 – 8 Minutes = 5.0 MPH
8 – 12 Minutes = 4.3 MPH
12 – 16 Minutes = 5.3 MPH
16 – 20 Minutes = 4.3 MPH
20 – 24 Minutes = 5.5 MPH
24 – 28 Minutes = 4.3 MPH
28 – 32 Minutes = 5.8 MPH
32 – 36 Minutes = 4.3 MPH
36 – 40 Minutes = 6.1 MPH
40 – 44 Minutes = 4.3 MPH
44 – 48 Minutes = 6.4 MPH
48 – 52 Minutes = 4.3 MPH
52 – 56 Minutes = 6.7 MPH

Example Male (3:40 26.2 Goal)

0 – 4 Minutes = 5.1 MPH
4 – 8 Minutes = 6.0 MPH
8 – 12 Minutes = 5.1 MPH
12 – 16 Minutes = 6.2 MPH
16 – 20 Minutes = 5.1 MPH
20 – 24 Minutes = 6.5 MPH
24 – 28 Minutes = 5.1 MPH
28 – 32 Minutes = 6.8 MPH
32 – 36 Minutes = 5.1 MPH
36 – 40 Minutes = 7.1 MPH
40 – 44 Minutes = 5.1 MPH
44 – 48 Minutes = 7.5 MPH
48 – 52 Minutes = 5.1 MPH
52 – 56 Minutes = 7.9 MPH

Let's Go Steady

1 Mile at 70% Marathon Pace

3 Miles at 100% Marathon Pace

1 Mile at 70% Marathon Pace

2 Miles at 100% Marathon Pace

TOTAL DISTANCE = 7 MILES

What you need to know for this workout:
70% Marathon Pace, 100% Marathon Pace

Example Female (4:00 26.2 Goal)	Example Male (3:30 26.2 Goal)
0 – 1 Mile = 5.0 MPH	0 – 1 Mile = 5.8 MPH
1 – 4 Miles = 6.6 MPH	1 – 4 Miles = 7.5 MPH
4 – 5 Miles = 5.0 MPH	4 – 5 Miles = 5.8 MPH
5 – 7 Miles = 6.6 MPH	5 – 7 Miles = 7.5 MPH

Just Keep Running

10 Minutes at 60% Marathon Pace

10 Minutes at 95% Marathon Pace

3 Minutes at 60% Marathon Pace

10 Minutes at 95% Marathon Pace

3 Minutes at 60% Marathon Pace

10 Minutes at 95% Marathon Pace

TOTAL DISTANCE = 4 - 6 MILES

What you need to know for this workout:
60% Marathon Pace, 95% Marathon Pace

Example Female (4:10 26.2 Goal)	Example Male (3:35 26.2 Goal)
0 – 10 Minutes = 4.5 MPH	0 – 10 Minutes = 5.2 MPH
10 – 20 Minutes = 6.0 MPH	10 – 20 Minutes = 7.3 MPH
20 – 23 Minutes = 4.5 MPH	20 – 23 Minutes = 5.2 MPH
23 – 33 Minutes = 6.0 MPH	23 – 33 Minutes = 7.3 MPH
33 – 36 Minutes = 4.5 MPH	33 – 36 Minutes = 5.2 MPH
36 – 46 Minutes = 6.0 MPH	36 – 46 Minutes = 7.3 MPH

~

Intermediate
5K to 10K Workouts

~

Intermediate 5K-10K

Female: training for a 5K with a personal best time of
22:30-28:00

Male: training for a 5K with a personal best time of
20:00-25:00

The workouts in this section are designed for 5K runners with a personal best time of 22:30-28 minutes for females, and 20-25 minutes for males.

Before each workout it is strongly recommended to do a warm up. After each workout it is highly advisable to perform cool down activities.

Each workout provides sample treadmill running paces based on your 5K goal pace. Additional 5K goal times and respective paces can be found in the charts section (located at the end of this book).

"It's very hard to understand in the beginning that the whole idea is not to beat the other runners. Eventually you learn that the competition is against the little voice inside you that wants to quit. "

12 * 400

1st, 2nd, 3rd, 4th 400 (.25 miles) with 30 Second break between 400's

5th, 6th, 7th, 8th 400 (.25 miles) with 60 Second break between 400's

9th, 10th, 11, 12th 400 (.25 miles) with 90 Second break between 400's

Start at Threshold pace

Increase .1 MPH in speed each 400 (.25 Miles)

TOTAL DISTANCE = 3 MILES

What you need to know for this workout:
Threshold Pace

Example Female (22:30 5K Goal)	Example Male (20:00 5K Goal)
0 - .25 Miles = 7.8 MPH	0 - .25 Miles = 8.7 MPH
.25 - .5 Miles = 7.9 MPH	.25 - .5 Miles = 8.8 MPH
.5 - .75 Miles = 8.0 MPH	.5 - .75 Miles = 8.9 MPH
.75 – 1.0 Mile = 8.1 MPH	.75 – 1.0 Mile = 9.0 MPH
1.0 – 1.25 Miles = 8.2 MPH	1.0 – 1.25 Miles = 9.1 MPH
1.25 – 1.5 Miles = 8.3 MPH	1.25 – 1.5 Miles = 9.2 MPH
1.5 – 1.75 Miles = 8.4 MPH	1.5 – 1.75 Miles = 9.3 MPH
1.75 – 2.0 Miles = 8.5 MPH	1.75 – 2.0 Miles = 9.4 MPH
2.0 – 2.25 Miles = 8.6 MPH	2.0 – 2.25 Miles = 9.5 MPH
2.25 – 2.5 Miles = 8.7 MPH	2.25 – 2.5 Miles = 9.6 MPH
2.5 – 2.75 Miles = 8.8 MPH	2.5 – 2.75 Miles = 9.7 MPH
2.75 – 3.0 Miles = 8.9 MPH	2.75 – 3.0 Miles = 9.8 MPH

15 * 1 Minute

:30 Seconds at 5K pace

:30 Seconds rest

Repeat Sequence 14 times (15 sequences total)

TOTAL DISTANCE = 1 - 1.5 MILES

What you need to know for this workout:
5K Pace

Example Female (23:00 5K Goal)

0 – :30 Sec. = 8.1 MPH Rest 30s
1 – 1:30 Min. = 8.1 MPH Rest 30s
2 – 2:30 Min. = 8.1 MPH Rest 30s
3 – 3:30 Min. = 8.1 MPH Rest 30s
4 – 4:30 Min. = 8.1 MPH Rest 30s
5 – 5:30 Min. = 8.1 MPH Rest 30s
6 – 6:30 Min. = 8.1 MPH Rest 30s
7 – 7:30 Min. = 8.1 MPH Rest 30s
8 – 8:30 Min. = 8.1 MPH Rest 30s
9 – 9:30 Min. = 8.1 MPH Rest 30s
10 – 10:30 Min. = 8.1 MPH Rest 30s
11 – 11:30 Min. = 8.1 MPH Rest 30s
12 – 12:30 Min. = 8.1 MPH Rest 30s
13– 13:30 Min. = 8.1 MPH Rest 30s
14 – 14:30 Min. = 8.1 MPH Rest 30s

Example Male (20:30 5K Goal)

0 – :30 Sec. = 9.1 MPH Rest 30s
1 – 1:30 Min. = 9.1 MPH Rest 30s
2 – 2:30 Min. = 9.1 MPH Rest 30s
3 – 3:30 Min. = 9.1 MPH Rest 30s
4 – 4:30 Min. = 9.1 MPH Rest 30s
5 – 5:30 Min. = 9.1 MPH Rest 30s
6 – 6:30 Min. = 9.1 MPH Rest 30s
7 – 7:30 Min. = 9.1 MPH Rest 30s
8 – 8:30 Min. = 9.1 MPH Rest 30s
9 – 9:30 Min. = 9.1 MPH Rest 30s
10 – 10:30 Min. = 9.1 MPH Rest 30s
11 – 11:30 Min. = 9.1 MPH Rest 30s
12 – 12:30 Min. = 9.1 MPH Rest 30s
13– 13:30 Min. = 9.1 MPH Rest 30s
14 – 14:30 Min. = 9.1 MPH Rest 30s

20 / 40

20 Seconds at 5K pace

40 Seconds at Marathon Pace

Repeat Sequence 19 times (20 sequences total)

TOTAL DISTANCE = 2.5 - 3 MILES

What you need to know for this workout:
5K Pace, Marathon Pace

Example Female (22:30 5K Goal)   Example Male (21:00 5K Goal)

0 – 20 Seconds = 7.9 MPH	0 – 20 Seconds = 8.9 MPH
20 – 60 Seconds = 7.0 MPH	20 – 60 Seconds = 7.8 MPH
1 – 1:20 Minutes = 7.9 MPH	1 – 1:20 Minutes = 8.9 MPH
1:20 – 2:00 Minutes = 7.0 MPH	1:20 – 2:00 Minutes = 7.8 MPH
2 – 2:20 Minutes = 7.9 MPH	2 – 2:20 Minutes = 8.9 MPH
2:20 – 3:00 Minutes = 7.0 MPH	2:20 – 3:00 Minutes = 7.8 MPH
3 – 3:20 Minutes = 7.9 MPH	3 – 3:20 Minutes = 8.9 MPH
3:20 – 4:00 Minutes = 7.0 MPH	3:20 – 4:00 Minutes = 7.8 MPH
4 – 4:20 Minutes = 7.9 MPH	4 – 4:20 Minutes = 8.9 MPH
4:20 – 5:00 Minutes = 7.0 MPH	4:20 – 5:00 Minutes = 7.8 MPH
5 – 5:20 Minutes = 7.9 MPH	5 – 5:20 Minutes = 8.9 MPH
5:20 – 6:00 Minutes = 7.0 MPH	5:20 – 6:00 Minutes = 7.8 MPH
6 – 6:20 Minutes = 7.9 MPH	6 – 6:20 Minutes = 8.9 MPH
6:20 – 7:00 Minutes = 7.0 MPH	6:20 – 7:00 Minutes = 7.8 MPH
7 – 7:20 Minutes = 7.9 MPH	7 – 7:20 Minutes = 8.9 MPH
7:20 – 8:00 Minutes = 7.0 MPH	7:20 – 8:00 Minutes = 7.8 MPH
8 – 8:20 Minutes = 7.9 MPH	8 – 8:20 Minutes = 8.9 MPH
8:20 – 9:00 Minutes = 7.0 MPH	8:20 – 9:00 Minutes = 7.8 MPH
9 – 9:20 Minutes = 7.9 MPH	9 – 9:20 Minutes = 8.9 MPH
9:20 – 10:00 Minutes = 7.0 MPH	9:20 – 10:00 Minutes = 7.8 MPH
10 – 10:20 Minutes = 7.9 MPH	10 – 10:20 Minutes = 8.9 MPH
10:20 – 11:00 Minutes = 7.0 MPH	10:20 – 11:00 Minutes = 7.8 MPH
11 – 11:20 Minutes = 7.9 MPH	11 – 11:20 Minutes = 8.9 MPH
11:20 – 12:00 Minutes = 7.0 MPH	11:20 – 12:00 Minutes = 7.8 MPH
12 – 12:20 Minutes = 7.9 MPH	12 – 12:20 Minutes = 8.9 MPH
12:20 – 13:00 Minutes = 7.0 MPH	12:20 – 13:00 Minutes = 7.8 MPH
13 – 13:20 Minutes = 7.9 MPH	13 – 13:20 Minutes = 8.9 MPH
13:20 – 14:00 Minutes = 7.0 MPH	13:20 – 14:00 Minutes = 7.8 MPH
14 – 14:20 Minutes = 7.9 MPH	14 – 14:20 Minutes = 8.9 MPH
14:20 – 15:00 Minutes = 7.0 MPH	14:20 – 15:00 Minutes = 7.8 MPH
15 – 15:20 Minutes = 7.9 MPH	15 – 15:20 Minutes = 8.9 MPH
15:20 – 16:00 Minutes = 7.0 MPH	15:20 – 16:00 Minutes = 7.8 MPH
16 – 16:20 Minutes = 7.9 MPH	16 – 16:20 Minutes = 8.9 MPH
16:20 – 17:00 Minutes = 7.0 MPH	16:20 – 17:00 Minutes = 7.8 MPH
17 – 17:20 Minutes = 7.9 MPH	17 – 17:20 Minutes = 8.9 MPH
17:20 – 18:00 Minutes = 7.0 MPH	17:20 – 18:00 Minutes = 7.8 MPH
18 – 18:20 Minutes = 7.9 MPH	18 – 18:20 Minutes = 8.9 MPH
18:20 – 19:00 Minutes = 7.0 MPH	18:20 – 19:00 Minutes = 7.8 MPH
19 – 19:20 Minutes = 7.9 MPH	19 – 19:20 Minutes = 8.9 MPH
19:20 – 20:00 Minutes = 7.0 MPH	19:20 – 20:00 Minutes = 7.8 MPH

Long and Hard

1 Mile at Marathon Pace

3 Miles at Threshold

1 Mile at Marathon Pace

TOTAL DISTANCE = 5 MILES

What you need to know for this workout:
Marathon Pace, Threshold Pace

Example Female (24:00 5K Goal)

0 – 1 Mile = 6.9 MPH
1 – 4 Miles = 7.4 MPH
4 – 5 Miles = 6.9 MPH

Example Male (21:30 5K Goal)

0 – 1 Mile = 7.6 MPH
1 – 4 Miles = 8.1 MPH
4 – 5 Miles = 7.6 MPH

Just One More

Start at Marathon Pace

Increase .1 MPH each minute until you cannot increase pace any longer

TOTAL DISTANCE = Unlimited MILES

What you need to know for this workout:
Marathon Pace

Example Female (24:30 5K Goal)

0 – 1 Minute = 6.8 MPH
Continue to Increase .1MPH each
MINUTE until failure

Example Male (22:00 5K Goal)

0 – 1 Minute = 7.5 MPH
Continue to Increase .1MPH each
MINUTE until failure

80 / 20 Rule

400 (.25 miles) at Marathon Pace

800 (.5 miles) at Threshold Pace

200 (.13 miles) at 1600 Pace

200 (.12 miles) at 1.0 MPH Slower than Marathon Pace

Repeat Sequence 2 additional times (3 sequences total)

TOTAL DISTANCE = 3 MILES

What you need to know for this workout:
Marathon Pace, Threshold Pace, 1600 Pace

Example Female (25:00 5K Goal)	Example Male (22:30 5K Goal)
0 - .25 Miles = 6.6 MPH	0 - .25 Miles = 7.3 MPH
.25 - .75 Miles = 7.1 MPH	.25 - .75 Miles = 7.8 MPH
.75 - .88 Miles = 7.8 MPH	.75 - .88 Miles = 8.7 MPH
.88 – 1.0 Miles = 5.6 MPH	.88 – 1.0 Miles = 6.3 MPH
1.00 - 1.25 Miles = 6.6 MPH	1.00 - 1.25 Miles = 7.3 MPH
1.25 - 1.75 Miles = 7.1 MPH	1.25 - 1.75 Miles = 7.8 MPH
1.75 - 1.88 Miles = 7.8 MPH	1.75 - 1.88 Miles = 8.7 MPH
1.88 – 2.0 Miles = 5.6 MPH	1.88 – 2.0 Miles = 6.3 MPH
2.00 - 2.25 Miles = 6.6 MPH	2.00 - 2.25 Miles = 7.3 MPH
2.25 - 2.75 Miles = 7.1 MPH	2.25 - 2.75 Miles = 7.8 MPH
2.75 - 2.88 Miles = 7.8 MPH	2.75 - 2.88 Miles = 8.7 MPH
2.88 – 3.0 Miles = 5.6 MPH	2.88 – 3.0 Miles = 6.3 MPH

Winners Challenge

9 Minutes starting at Marathon Pace

Increase .1 MPH each 45 seconds until 9 minutes

Repeat Sequence (2 sequences total)

TOTAL DISTANCE = 1.5 - 2.5 MILES

What you need to know for this workout:
Marathon Pace

Example Female (25:30 5K Goal)	Example Male (23:00 5K Goal)
0 – :45 Seconds = 6.5 MPH	0 – :45 Seconds = 7.2 MPH
:45 – 1:30 Minutes = 6.6 MPH	:45 – 1:30 Minutes = 7.3 MPH
1:30 – 2:15 Minutes = 6.7 MPH	1:30 – 2:15 Minutes = 7.4 MPH
2:15 – 3:00 Minutes = 6.8 MPH	2:15 – 3:00 Minutes = 7.5 MPH
3:00 – 3:45 Minutes = 6.9 MPH	3:00 – 3:45 Minutes = 7.6 MPH
3:45 – 4:30 Minutes = 7.0 MPH	3:45 – 4:30 Minutes = 7.7 MPH
4:30 – 5:15 Minutes = 7.1 MPH	4:30 – 5:15 Minutes = 7.8 MPH
5:15 – 6:00 Minutes = 7.2 MPH	5:15 – 6:00 Minutes = 7.9 MPH
6:00 – 6:45 Minutes = 7.3 MPH	6:00 – 6:45 Minutes = 8.0 MPH
6:45 – 7:30 Minutes = 7.4 MPH	6:45 – 7:30 Minutes = 8.1 MPH
7:30 – 8:15 Minutes = 7.5 MPH	7:30 – 8:15 Minutes = 8.1 MPH
8:15 – 9:00 Minutes = 7.6 MPH	8:15 – 9:00 Minutes = 8.2 MPH
Repeat	Repeat

Lost My Breakfast

.1 Mile at 5k Pace

.9 Miles at Marathon Pace

.2 Miles at 5k pace

.8 Miles at Marathon Pace

.3 Miles at 5K pace

.7 Miles at Marathon Pace

.4 Miles at 5K pace

.6 Miles at Marathon Pace

.5 Miles at 5K pace

.5 Miles at Marathon Pace

TOTAL DISTANCE = 5 MILES

What you need to know for this workout:
Marathon Pace, 5K Pace

Example Female (26:00 5K Goal)	Example Male (23:30 5K Goal)
0 - .1 Miles = 7.2 MPH	0 - .1 Miles = 7.9 MPH
.1 – 1.0 Mile = 6.4 MPH	.1 – 1.0 Mile = 7.0 MPH
1.0 – 1.2 Miles = 7.2 MPH	1.0 – 1.2 Miles = 7.9 MPH
1.2 – 2.0 Miles = 6.4 MPH	1.2 – 2.0 Miles = 7.0 MPH
2.0 – 2.3 Miles = 7.2 MPH	2.0 – 2.3 Miles = 7.9 MPH
2.3 – 3.0 Miles = 6.4 MPH	2.3 – 3.0 Miles = 7.0 MPH
3.0 – 3.4 Miles = 7.2 MPH	3.0 – 3.4 Miles = 7.9 MPH
3.4 – 4.0 Miles = 6.4 MPH	3.4 – 4.0 Miles = 7.0 MPH
4.0 – 4.5 Miles = 7.2 MPH	4.0 – 4.5 Miles = 7.9 MPH
4.5 – 5.0 Miles = 6.4 MPH	4.5 – 5.0 Miles = 7.0 MPH

Recover and Go

1.0 Mile at Marathon Pace

.75 Miles at Threshold Pace

.5 Miles at 10K Pace

.25 Miles at 5k Pace

TOTAL DISTANCE = 2.5 MILES

What you need to know for this workout:
Marathon Pace, Threshold Pace, 10K Pace, 5K Pace

Example Female (26:30 5K Goal)

0 – 1.0 Mile = 6.9 MPH
1.0 – 1.75 Miles = 6.7 MPH
1.75 – 2.25 Miles = 6.8 MPH
2.25 – 2.5 Miles = 7.0 MPH

Example Male (24:00 5K Goal)

0 – 1.0 Mile = 6.9 MPH
1.0 – 1.75 Miles = 7.4 MPH
1.75 – 2.25 Miles = 7.5 MPH
2.25 – 2.5 Miles = 7.7 MPH

Steady Wins the Race

400 (.25 Miles) at Marathon Pace

400 (.25 Miles) at 10k Pace

Repeat Sequence 9 additional times (10 sequences total)

TOTAL DISTANCE = 5 MILES

What you need to know for this workout:
Marathon Pace, 10K Pace

Example Female (27:00 5K Goal)	Example Male (24:30 5K Goal)
0 - .25 Miles = 6.2 MPH	0 - .25 Miles = 6.8 MPH
.25 - .5 Miles = 6.7 MPH	.25 - .5 Miles = 7.3 MPH
.5 - .75 Miles = 6.2 MPH	.5 - .75 Miles = 6.8 MPH
.75 – 1.0 Mile = 6.7 MPH	.75 – 1.0 Mile = 7.3 MPH
1.0 – 1.25 Miles = 6.2 MPH	1.0 – 1.25 Miles = 6.8 MPH
1.25 – 1.5 Miles = 6.7 MPH	1.25 – 1.5 Miles = 7.3 MPH
1.5 – 1.75 Miles = 6.2 MPH	1.5 – 1.75 Miles = 6.8 MPH
1.75 – 2.0 Miles = 6.7 MPH	1.75 – 2.0 Miles = 7.3 MPH
2.0 – 2.25 Miles = 6.2 MPH	2.0 – 2.25 Miles = 6.8 MPH
2.25 – 2.5 Miles = 6.7 MPH	2.25 – 2.5 Miles = 7.3 MPH
2.5 – 2.75 Miles = 6.2 MPH	2.5 – 2.75 Miles = 6.8 MPH
2.75 – 3.0 Miles = 6.7 MPH	2.75 – 3.0 Miles = 7.3 MPH
3.0 – 3.25 Miles = 6.2 MPH	3.0 – 3.25 Miles = 6.8 MPH
3.25 – 3.5 Miles = 6.7 MPH	3.25 – 3.5 Miles = 7.3 MPH
3.5 – 3.75 Miles = 6.2 MPH	3.5 – 3.75 Miles = 6.8 MPH
3.75 – 4.0 Miles = 6.7 MPH	3.75 – 4.0 Miles = 7.3 MPH
4.0 – 4.25 Miles = 6.2 MPH	4.0 – 4.25 Miles = 6.8 MPH
4.25 – 4.5 Miles = 6.7 MPH	4.25 – 4.5 Miles = 7.3 MPH
4.5 – 4.75 Miles = 6.2 MPH	4.5 – 4.75 Miles = 6.8 MPH
4.75 – 5.0 Miles = 6.7 MPH	4.75 – 5.0 Miles = 7.3 MPH

~
Intermediate
½ Marathon Workouts
~

Intermediate ½ Marathon

Female: training for a ½ Marathon with a personal best time of 1 hour and 45 minutes to 2 hours

Male: training for a ½ Marathon with a personal best time of 1 hour and 30 minutes to 1 hour and forty-five minutes

The workouts in this section are designed for ½ Marathon runners with a personal best time of 1:45-2 hours for females, and 1:30-1:45 for males.

Before each workout it is strongly recommended to do a warm up. After each workout it is highly advisable to perform cool down activities.

Each workout provides sample treadmill running paces based on your ½ Marathon goal pace. Additional ½ Marathon goal times and respective paces can be found in the charts section (located at the end of this book).

"There is no one giant step that does it, it's a lot of little steps. "

800's

8 by 800 (.5 miles) at descending pace

Start at Half Marathon Pace

Gradually Increase each 800 (.5 miles) until you reach 5K Pace

Continue 5K Pace for the remainder of the workout

Rest 2 Minutes between 800's (.5 miles)

TOTAL DISTANCE = 4 MILES

What you need to know for this workout:
Half Marathon Pace, 5K Pace

Example Female (1:45 13.1 Goal)	Example Male (1:30 13.1 Goal)
0-.5 Miles = 7.5 MPH	0-.5 Miles = 8.7 MPH
Rest 2 Minutes	Rest 2 Minutes
.5 - 1.0 Mile = 7.6 MPH	.5 -1.0 Mile = 8.8 MPH
Rest 2 Minutes	Rest 2 Minutes
1.0 – 1.5 Miles = 7.7 MPH	1.0 – 1.5 Miles = 8.9 MPH
Rest 2 Minutes	Rest 2 Minutes
1.5 – 2.0 Miles = 7.8 MPH	1.5 – 2.0 Miles = 9.0 MPH
Rest 2 Minutes	Rest 2 Minutes
2.0 – 2.5 Miles = 7.9 MPH	2.0 – 2.5 Miles = 9.1 MPH
Rest 2 Minutes	Rest 2 Minutes
2.5 – 3.0 Miles = 8.0 MPH	2.5 – 3.0 Miles = 9.3 MPH
Rest 2 Minutes	Rest 2 Minutes
3.0 – 3.5 Miles = 8.1 MPH	3.0 – 3.5 Miles = 9.4 MPH
Rest 2 Minutes	Rest 2 Minutes
3.5 – 4.0 Miles = 8.1 MPH	3.5 – 4.0 Miles = 9.5 MPH

Tempo Day

2 Miles at Marathon Pace

1 Mile at Threshold Pace

1 Mile at Marathon Pace

4 Miles at Half Marathon Pace

1 Mile at Marathon Pace

1 Mile at 10K Pace

TOTAL DISTANCE = 10 MILES

What you need to know for this workout:
Marathon Pace, Threshold Pace, Half Marathon Pace, 10K Pace

Example Female (1:50 13.1 Goal)	Example Male (1:35 13.1 Goal)
0 – 2.0 Miles = 6.9 MPH	0 – 2.0 Miles = 8.0 MPH
2.0 – 3.0 Miles = 7.4 MPH	2.0 – 3.0 Miles = 8.5 MPH
3.0 – 4.0 Miles = 6.9 MPH	3.0 – 4.0 Miles = 8.0 MPH
4.0 – 8.0 Miles = 7.2 MPH	4.0 – 8.0 Miles = 8.3 MPH
8.0 – 9.0 Miles = 6.9 MPH	8.0 – 9.0 Miles = 8.0 MPH
9.0 – 10.0 Miles = 7.5 MPH	9.0 – 10.0 Miles = 8.7 MPH

Up and Down

2 Miles at Marathon Pace

2 Miles at Half Marathon Pace

2 Miles at Marathon Pace

2 Miles at Half Marathon Pace

Half Marathon Pace miles are run at 1% incline

Marathon Pace miles are run at 2% incline

TOTAL DISTANCE = 8 MILES

What you need to know for this workout:
Marathon Pace, Half Marathon Pace

Example Female (1:55 13.1 Goal)

0 – 2.0 Miles = 6.6 MPH @ 2% Incline
2.0 – 4.0 Miles = 6.8 MPH @ 1% Incl.
4.0 – 6.0 Miles = 6.6 MPH @ 2% Incl.
6.0 – 8.0 Miles = 6.8 MPH @ 1% Incl.

Example Male (1:40 13.1 Goal)

0 – 2.0 Miles = 7.6 MPH @ 2% Incline
2.0 – 4.0 Miles = 7.9 MPH @ 1% Incl.
4.0 – 6.0 Miles = 7.6 MPH @ 2% Incl.
6.0 – 8.0 Miles = 7.9 MPH @ 1% Incl.

400 Day

10 by 400 (.25 miles) at 5K pace

Jog 400 (.25 miles) at 1 MPH slower than Marathon Pace between 400's

Repeat 9 Additional Sequences (10 Sequences total)

TOTAL DISTANCE = 5 MILES

What you need to know for this workout:
Marathon Pace, 5K Pace

Example Female (2:00 13.1 Goal)	Example Male (1:45 13.1 Goal)
0 - .25 Miles = 7.2 MPH	0 - .25 Miles = 8.1 MPH
.25 - .50 Miles = 5.4 MPH	.25 - .5 Miles = 6.2 MPH
.50 - .75 Miles = 7.2 MPH	.5 - .75 Miles = 8.1 MPH
.75 – 1.0 Mile = 5.4 MPH	.75 – 1.0 Mile = 6.2 MPH
1.0 – 1.25 Miles = 7.2 MPH	1.0 – 1.25 Miles = 8.1 MPH
1.25 – 1.5 Miles = 5.4 MPH	1.25 – 1.5 Miles = 6.2 MPH
1.5 – 1.75 Miles = 7.2 MPH	1.5 – 1.75 Miles = 8.1 MPH
1.75 – 2.0 Miles = 5.4 MPH	1.75 – 2.0 Miles = 6.2 MPH
2.0 – 2.25 Miles = 7.2 MPH	2.0 – 2.25 Miles = 8.1 MPH
2.25 – 2.5 Miles = 5.4 MPH	2.25 – 2.5 Miles = 6.2 MPH
2.5 – 2.75 Miles = 7.2 MPH	2.5 – 2.75 Miles = 8.1 MPH
2.75 – 3.0 Miles = 5.4 MPH	2.75 – 3.0 Miles = 6.2 MPH
3.0 – 3.25 Miles = 7.2 MPH	3.0 – 3.25 Miles = 8.1 MPH
3.25 – 3.5 Miles = 5.4 MPH	3.25 – 3.5 Miles = 6.2 MPH
3.5 – 3.75 Miles = 7.2 MPH	3.5 – 3.75 Miles = 8.1 MPH
3.75 – 4.0 Miles = 5.4 MPH	3.75 – 4.0 Miles = 6.2 MPH
4.0 – 4.25 Miles = 7.2 MPH	4.0 – 4.25 Miles = 8.1 MPH
4.25 – 4.5 Miles = 5.4 MPH	4.25 – 4.5 Miles = 6.2 MPH
4.5 – 4.75 Miles = 7.2 MPH	4.5 – 4.75 Miles = 8.1 MPH
4.75 – 5.0 Miles = 5.4 MPH	4.75 – 5.0 Miles = 6.2 MPH

Steady Pace

10 Minutes at 1 MPH slower than Marathon Pace

20 Minutes at Half Marathon Pace

10 Minutes at Marathon Pace

15 Minutes at Half Marathon Pace

TOTAL DISTANCE = 7 - 8.5 MILES

What you need to know for this workout:
Marathon Pace, Half Marathon Pace

Example Female (1:45 13.1 Goal)	Example Male (1:30 13.1 Goal)
0 – 10 Minutes = 6.2 MPH	0 – 10 Minutes = 7.4 MPH
10 – 30 Minutes = 7.5 MPH	10 – 30 Minutes = 8.7 MPH
30 – 40 Minutes = 7.2 MPH	30 – 40 Minutes = 8.4 MPH
40 – 55 Minutes = 7.5 MPH	40 – 55 Minutes = 8.7 MPH

Let's Run

10 Minutes at 1 MPH slower than Marathon Pace

45 Minutes at Marathon Pace

5 Minutes at 1 MPH slower than Marathon Pace

15 Minutes at Half Marathon Pace

TOTAL DISTANCE = 8 - 10 MILES

What you need to know for this workout:
Marathon Pace, Half Marathon Pace

Example Female (1:50 13.1 Goal)	Example Male (1:35 13.1 Goal)
0 – 10 Minutes = 5.9 MPH	0 – 10 Minutes = 7.0 MPH
10 – 55 Minutes = 6.9 MPH	10 – 55 Minutes = 8.0 MPH
55 – 60 Minutes = 5.9 MPH	55 – 60 Minutes = 7.0 MPH
60 – 75 Minutes = 7.2 MPH	60 – 75 Minutes = 8.3 MPH

Pace Changes

5 Minutes at Marathon Pace

5 Minutes at Half Marathon Pace

5 Minutes at Threshold Pace

5 Minutes at 10K Pace

2 Minutes at 5K Pace

Rest 5 Minutes between sequences

Repeat Sequence

TOTAL DISTANCE = 4.5 - 6.5 MILES

What you need to know for this workout:
Marathon Pace, Half Marathon Pace, Threshold Pace, 10K Pace,
5K Pace

Example Female (1:55 13.1 Goal)

0 – 5 Minutes = 6.6 MPH
5 – 10 Minutes = 6.8 MPH
10 – 15 Minutes = 7.1 MPH
15 – 20 Minutes = 7.2 MPH
20 – 22 Minutes = 7.4 MPH
Rest 5 Minutes
Repeat

Example Male (1:40 13.1 Goal)

0 – 5 Minutes = 7.6 MPH
5 – 10 Minutes = 7.9 MPH
10 – 15 Minutes = 8.1 MPH
15 – 20 Minutes = 8.3 MPH
20 – 22 Minutes = 8.6 MPH
Rest 5 Minutes
Repeat

10 K Time Trial

Start at Marathon Pace

Increase gradually until you reach 10K pace

Record total time to complete 10K

Be sure to increase gradually during the workout.

Workout can be completed multiple times during training cycle to gauge fitness.

TOTAL DISTANCE = 6.2 MILES

What you need to know for this workout:
Marathon Pace, 10K Pace

Example Female (2:00 13.1 Goal)	Example Male (1:45 13.1 Goal)
Start at 6.4 MPH	Start at 7.2 MPH
Slowly Increase to 6.9 MPH	Slowly Increase to 7.9 MPH
and hold for 6.2 Miles	and hold for 6.2 Miles
Record Time	Record Time

Mile On Mile Off

1 Mile at Marathon Pace

1 Mile at Half Marathon Pace

Repeat Sequence 3 additional times (4 sequences total)

TOTAL DISTANCE = 8 MILES

What you need to know for this workout:
Marathon Pace, Half Marathon Pace

Example Female (1:45 13.1 Goal)	Example Male (1:30 13.1 Goal)
0 – 1 Mile = 7.2 MPH	0 – 1 Mile = 8.4 MPH
1 – 2 Miles = 7.5 MPH	1 – 2 Miles = 8.7 MPH
2 – 3 Miles = 7.2 MPH	2 – 3 Miles = 8.4 MPH
3 – 4 Miles = 7.5 MPH	3 – 4 Miles = 8.7 MPH
4 – 5 Miles = 7.2 MPH	4 – 5 Miles = 8.4 MPH
5 – 6 Miles = 7.5 MPH	5 – 6 Miles = 8.7 MPH
6 – 7 Miles = 7.2 MPH	6 – 7 Miles = 8.4 MPH
7 – 8 Miles = 7.5 MPH	7 – 8 Miles = 8.7 MPH

Hold It

1 Mile at 1.0 MPH Slower than Marathon Pace

3 Miles at Threshold Pace

1 Mile at 1.0 MPH slower than Marathon Pace

3 Miles at Half Marathon Pace

TOTAL DISTANCE = 8 MILES

What you need to know for this workout:
Marathon Pace, Half Marathon Pace, Threshold Pace

Example Female (1:50 13.1 Goal)

0 – 1 Mile = 5.9 MPH
1 – 4 Miles = 7.4 MPH
4 – 5 Miles = 5.9 MPH
5 – 8 Miles = 7.2 MPH

Example Male (1:35 13.1 Goal)

0 – 1 Mile = 7.0 MPH
1 – 4 Miles = 8.5 MPH
4 – 5 Miles = 7.0 MPH
5 – 8 Miles = 8.3 MPH

~

Intermediate
Marathon Workouts

~

Intermediate Marathon

Female: training for a Marathon with a personal best time of 3 hours and 24 minutes to 4 hours

Male: training for a Marathon with a personal best time of 3 hours to 3 hours and 30 minutes

The workouts in this section are designed for Marathon runners with a personal best time of 3:24-4:00 hours for females, and 3:00 – 3:30 for males.

Before each workout it is strongly recommended to do a warm up. After each workout it is highly advisable to perform cool down activities.

Each workout provides sample treadmill running paces based on your Marathon goal pace. Additional Marathon goal times and respective paces can be found in the charts section (located at the end of this book).

"There will be days when you don't know if you can run a marathon, there will be a lifetime of knowing you have. "

4 * Mile

Mile 1 at 105% Marathon pace

Mile 2 at 110% Marathon Pace

Mile 3 at 115% Marathon Pace

Mile 4 at 120% Marathon Pace

Rest 3-4 Minutes between Miles

TOTAL DISTANCE = 4 MILES

What you need to know for this workout:
105% Marathon Pace, 110% Marathon Pace, 115% Marathon Pace, 120% Marathon Pace

Example Female (3:30 26.2 Goal)	Example Male (3:00 26.2 Goal)
0 – 1 Mile = 7.9 MPH	0 – 1 Mile = 9.2 MPH
Rest 3 Minutes	Rest 3 Minutes
1 – 2 Miles = 8.3 MPH	1 – 2 Miles = 9.7 MPH
Rest 3 Minutes	Rest 3 Minutes
2 – 3 Miles = 8.8 MPH	2 – 3 Miles = 10.2 MPH
Rest 3 Minutes	Rest 3 Minutes
3 – 4 Miles = 9.4 MPH	3 – 4 Miles = 10.9 MPH

6 Mile Change of Pace

Start at 70% Marathon Pace for .5 Miles

Alternate between 70% Marathon Pace and 100% Marathon Pace every .5 Miles

TOTAL DISTANCE = 6 MILES

What you need to know for this workout:
70% Marathon Pace, 100% Marathon Pace

Example Female (3:35 26.2 Goal)	Example Male (3:05 26.2 Goal)
0 - .5 Miles = 5.6 MPH	0 - .5 Miles = 6.5 MPH
.5 – 1.0 Mile = 7.3 MPH	.5 – 1.0 Mile = 8.5 MPH
1.0 – 1.5 Miles = 5.6 MPH	1.0 – 1.5 Miles = 6.5 MPH
1.5 – 2.0 Miles = 7.3 MPH	1.5 – 2.0 Miles = 8.5 MPH
2.0 – 2.5 Miles = 5.6 MPH	2.0 – 2.5 Miles = 6.5 MPH
2.5 – 3.0 Miles = 7.3 MPH	2.5 – 3.0 Miles = 8.5 MPH
3.0 – 3.5 Miles = 5.6 MPH	3.0 – 3.5 Miles = 6.5 MPH
3.5 – 4.0 Miles = 7.3 MPH	3.5 – 4.0 Miles = 8.5 MPH
4.0 – 4.5 Miles = 5.6 MPH	4.0 – 4.5 Miles = 6.5 MPH
4.5 – 5.0 Miles = 7.3 MPH	4.5 – 5.0 Miles = 8.5 MPH
5.0 – 5.5 Miles = 5.6 MPH	5.0 – 5.5 Miles = 6.5 MPH
5.5 – 6.0 Miles = 7.3 MPH	5.5 – 6.0 Miles = 8.5 MPH

Hill Day

80% Marathon Pace with Incline at 1% for 1 Mile

Increase the incline 1% each .25 miles until 4%

Repeat incline sequence for 4 miles

Final 1 Mile at 80% Marathon Pace with 1% incline

TOTAL DISTANCE = 5 MILES

What you need to know for this workout:
80% Marathon Pace

Example Female (3:40 26.2 Goal)	Example Male (3:10 26.2 Goal)
0 – 1 Mile = 6.0 MPH 1% Incline	0 – 1 Mile = 6.9 MPH 1% Incline
1.0 – 1.25 Miles = 6.0 MPH 1% Incline	1.0 – 1.25 Miles = 6.9 MPH 1% Incline
1.25 – 1.5 Miles = 6.0 MPH 2% Incline	1.25 – 1.5 Miles = 6.9 MPH 2% Incline
1.5 – 1.75 Miles = 6.0 MPH 3% Incline	1.5 – 1.75 Miles = 6.9 MPH 3% Incline
1.75 – 2.0 Miles = 6.0 MPH 4% Incline	1.75 – 2.0 Miles = 6.9 MPH 4% Incline
2.0 – 2.25 Miles = 6.0 MPH 1% Incline	2.0 – 2.25 Miles = 6.9 MPH 1% Incline
2.25 – 2.5 Miles = 6.0 MPH 2% Incline	2.25 – 2.5 Miles = 6.9 MPH 2% Incline
2.5 – 2.75 Miles = 6.0 MPH 3% Incline	2.5 – 2.75 Miles = 6.9 MPH 3% Incline
2.75 – 3.0 Miles = 6.0 MPH 4% Incline	2.75 – 3.0 Miles = 6.9 MPH 4% Incline
3.0 – 3.25 Miles = 6.0 MPH 1% Incline	3.0 – 3.25 Miles = 6.9 MPH 1% Incline
3.25 – 3.5 Miles = 6.0 MPH 2% Incline	3.25 – 3.5 Miles = 6.9 MPH 2% Incline
3.5 – 3.75 Miles = 6.0 MPH 3% Incline	3.5 – 3.75 Miles = 6.9 MPH 3% Incline
3.75 – 4.0 Miles = 6.0 MPH 4% Incline	3.75 – 4.0 Miles = 6.9 MPH 4% Incline
4.0 – 5.0 Miles = 6.0 MPH 1% Incline	4.0 – 5.0 Miles = 6.9 MPH 1% Incline

Marathon Simulation Long Day

1 Mile at 60% Marathon Pace

1 Mile at 70% Marathon Pace

1 Mile at 75% Marathon Pace

1 Mile at 80% Marathon Pace

1 Mile at 85% Marathon Pace

3 Miles at 90% Marathon Pace

1 Mile at 60 % Marathon Pace

1 Mile at 100% Marathon Pace

TOTAL DISTANCE = 10 MILES

What you need to know for this workout:
60% Marathon Pace, 70% Marathon Pace, 75% Marathon Pace,
80% Marathon Pace, 85% Marathon Pace, 90% Marathon Pace,
100% Marathon Pace

Example Female (3:45 26.2 Goal)	Example Male (3:15 26.2 Goal)
0 – 1.0 Mile = 5.0 MPH	0 – 1.0 Mile = 5.8 MPH
1.0 – 2.0 Miles = 5.4 MPH	1.0 – 2.0 Miles = 6.2 MPH
2.0 – 3.0 Miles = 5.6 MPH	2.0 – 3.0 Miles = 6.5 MPH
3.0 – 4.0 Miles = 5.8 MPH	3.0 – 4.0 Miles = 6.7 MPH
4.0 – 5.0 Miles = 6.1 MPH	4.0 – 5.0 Miles = 7.0 MPH
5.0 – 8.0 Miles = 6.4 MPH	5.0 – 8.0 Miles = 7.3 MPH
8.0 – 9.0 Miles = 5.0 MPH	8.0 – 9.0 Miles = 5.8 MPH
9.0 – 10.0 Miles = 7.0 MPH	9.0 – 10.0 Miles = 8.1 MPH

Steady State Workout

10 Minutes at 70% Marathon Pace

25 Minutes at 100% Marathon Pace

10 Minutes at 75% Marathon Pace

TOTAL DISTANCE = 4 - 6 MILES

What you need to know for this workout:
70% Marathon Pace, 75% Marathon Pace, 100% Marathon Pace

Example Female (3:50 26.2 Goal)	Example Male (3:20 26.2 Goal)
0 – 10 Minutes = 5.3 MPH	0 – 10 Minutes = 6.1 MPH
10 – 35 Minutes = 6.8 MPH	10 – 35 Minutes = 7.9 MPH
35 – 45 Minutes = 5.5 MPH	35 – 45 Minutes = 6.3 MPH

<u>Pyramid Training</u>

5 Minutes at 70% Marathon Pace

5 Minutes at 120% Marathon Pace

5 Minutes at 75% Marathon Pace

5 Minutes at 115% Marathon Pace

5 Minutes at 80% Marathon Pace

5 Minutes at 110% Marathon Pace

5 Minutes at 85% Marathon Pace

5 Minutes at 105% Marathon Pace

5 Minutes at 90% Marathon Pace

5 Minutes at 100% Marathon Pace

5 Minutes at 95% Marathon Pace

TOTAL DISTANCE = 5.5 - 7.5 MILES

What you need to know for this workout:
70% Marathon Pace, 75% Marathon Pace, 80% Marathon Pace,
85% Marathon Pace, 90% Marathon Pace, 95% Marathon Pace,
100% Marathon Pace

Example Female (3:55 26.2 Goal)

0 – 5 Minutes = 5.2 MPH
5 – 10 Minutes = 8.3 MPH
10 – 15 Minutes = 5.4 MPH
15 – 20 Minutes = 7.8 MPH
20 – 25 Minutes = 5.6 MPH
25 – 30 Minutes = 7.4 MPH
30 – 35 Minutes = 5.8 MPH
35 – 40 Minutes = 7.0 MPH
40 – 45 Minutes = 6.1 MPH
45 – 50 Minutes = 6.7 MPH
50 – 55 Minutes = 6.4 MPH

Example Male (3:25 26.2 Goal)

0 – 5 Minutes = 5.9 MPH
5 – 10 Minutes = 9.5 MPH
10 – 15 Minutes = 6.1 MPH
15 – 20 Minutes = 8.9 MPH
20 – 25 Minutes = 6.4 MPH
25 – 30 Minutes = 8.5 MPH
30 – 35 Minutes = 6.7 MPH
35 – 40 Minutes = 8.1 MPH
40 – 45 Minutes = 7.0 MPH
45 – 50 Minutes = 7.7 MPH
50 – 55 Minutes = 7.3 MPH

Test Yourself

Begin running at 60% Marathon Pace

Gradually increase your pace until you are running at 100% Marathon Pace

Once running at Marathon Pace – continue for 3 Miles

Workout Length will vary depending on the length of time to reach Marathon Pace.

Be patient and resist increasing speed too quickly

TOTAL DISTANCE = Various MILES

What you need to know for this workout:
60% Marathon Pace, 100% Marathon Pace

Example Female (4:00 26.2 Goal)

Begin at 4.7 MPH
Slowly Increase pace to 6.6 MPH
Hold 6.6 MPH Pace for 3 Miles

Example Male (3:30 26.2 Goal)

Begin at 5.3 MPH
Slowly Increase Pace to 7.5 MPH
Hold 7.5 MPH Pace for 3 Miles

4 Part Long Run

3 Miles at 70% Marathon Pace

3 Miles at 80% Marathon Pace

3 Miles at 85% Marathon Pace

3 Miles at 90% Marathon Pace (depending on fatigue level, final mile may increase to 100% marathon pace)

TOTAL DISTANCE = 12 MILES

What you need to know for this workout:
70% Marathon Pace, 80% Marathon Pace, 85% Marathon Pace,
90% Marathon Pace, 100% Marathon Pace

Example Female (3:40 26.2 Goal)   **Example Male (3:15 26.2 Goal)**

0 – 3 Miles = 5.5 MPH	0 – 3 Miles = 6.2 MPH
3 – 6 Miles = 6.0 MPH	3 – 6 Miles = 6.7 MPH
6 – 9 Miles = 6.2 MPH	6 – 9 Miles = 7.0 MPH
9 – 12 Miles = 6.5 MPH	9 – 12 Miles = 7.3 MPH

10K Training Run

1 Mile at 80% Marathon Pace

.5 Miles at 120% Marathon Pace

1 Mile at 80% Marathon pace

.5 Miles at 115% Marathon Pace

1 Mile at 80% Marathon Pace

.5 Miles at 110% Marathon pace

1 Mile at 80% Marathon Pace

.5 Miles at 105% Marathon Pace

.2 Miles at 100% Marathon pace

TOTAL DISTANCE = 6.2 MILES

What you need to know for this workout:
80% Marathon Pace, 100% Marathon Pace, 105% Marathon Pace, 110% Marathon Pace, 115% Marathon Pace, 120% Marathon Pace

Example Female (3:30 26.2 Goal)	Example Male (3:10 26.2 Goal)
0 – 1 Mile = 6.2 MPH	0 – 1 Miles = 6.9 MPH
1 – 1.5 Miles = 9.4 MPH	1 – 1.5 Miles = 10.3 MPH
1.5 – 2.5 Miles = 6.2 MPH	1.5 – 2.5 Miles = 6.9 MPH
2.5 – 3.0 Miles = 8.8 MPH	2.5 – 3.0 Miles = 9.8 MPH
3.0 – 4.0 Miles = 6.2 MPH	3.0 – 4.0 Miles = 6.9 MPH
4.0 – 4.5 Miles = 8.3 MPH	4.0 – 4.5 Miles = 9.2 MPH
4.5 – 5.5 Miles= 6.2 MPH	4.5 – 5.5 Miles = 6.9 MPH
5.5 – 6.0 Miles = 7.9 MPH	5.5 – 6.0 Miles = 8.7 MPH
6.0 – 6.2 Miles = 7.5 MPH	6.0 – 6.2 Miles = 8.3 MPH

All About Marathon Pace

.25 Miles at 75% Marathon Pace

.25 Miles at Marathon Pace

Continue for 5 Miles

TOTAL DISTANCE = 5 MILES

What you need to know for this workout:
75% Marathon Pace, 100% Marathon Pace

Example Female (3:50 26.2 Goal)	Example Male (3:25 26.2 Goal)
0 - .25 Miles = 5.5 MPH	0 - .25 Miles = 6.1 MPH
.25 - .5 Miles = 6.8 MPH	.25 - .5 Miles = 7.7 MPH
.5 - .75 Miles = 5.5 MPH	.5 - .75 Miles = 6.1 MPH
.75 – 1.0 Miles = 6.8 MPH	.75 – 1.0 Mile = 7.7 MPH
1.0 – 1.25 Miles = 5.5 MPH	1.0 – 1.25 Miles = 6.1 MPH
1.25 – 1.5 Miles = 6.8 MPH	1.25 – 1.5 Miles = 7.7 MPH
1.5 – 1.75 Miles = 5.5 MPH	1.5 – 1.75 Miles = 6.1 MPH
1.75 – 2.0 Miles = 6.8 MPH	1.75 – 2.0 Miles = 7.7 MPH
2.0 – 2.25 Miles = 5.5 MPH	2.0 – 2.25 Miles = 6.1 MPH
2.25 – 2.5 Miles = 6.8 MPH	2.25 – 2.5 Miles = 7.7 MPH
2.5 – 2.75 Miles = 5.5 MPH	2.5 – 2.75 Miles = 6.1 MPH
2.75 – 3.0 Miles = 6.8 MPH	2.75 – 3.0 Miles = 7.7 MPH
3.0 – 3.25 Miles = 5.5 MPH	3.0 – 3.25 Miles = 6.1 MPH
3.25 – 3.5 Miles = 6.8 MPH	3.25 – 3.5 Miles = 7.7 MPH
3.5 – 3.75 Miles = 5.5 MPH	3.5 – 3.75 Miles = 6.1 MPH
3.75 – 4.0 Miles = 6.8 MPH	3.75 – 4.0 Miles = 7.7 MPH
4.0 – 4.25 Miles = 5.5 MPH	4.0 – 4.25 Miles = 6.1 MPH
4.25 – 4.5 Miles = 6.8 MPH	4.25 – 4.5 Miles = 7.7 MPH
4.5 – 4.75 Miles = 5.5 MPH	4.5 – 4.75 Miles = 6.1 MPH
4.75 – 5.0 Miles = 6.8 MPH	4.75 – 5.0 Miles = 7.7 MPH

~

Advanced
5K to 10K Workouts

~

Advanced 5K-10K

Female: training for a 5K-10K with a personal best 5K time below 22 minutes and 30 seconds

Male: training for a 5K-10K with a personal best 5K time below 20 minutes

The workouts in this section are designed for 5K-10K runners with a personal best time below 22 minutes and 30 seconds for females, and below 20 minutes for males.

Before each workout it is strongly recommended to do a warm up. After each workout it is highly advisable to perform cool down activities.

Each workout provides sample treadmill running paces based on your 5K-10K goal pace. Additional 5K-10K goal times and respective paces can be found in the charts section (located at the end of this book).

"Your body can stand almost anything. It's your mind you have to convince."

20 Minute Time Trial

Start at Marathon Pace then increase throughout the run

Run for 20 Minutes

Goal is to finish at 5K Pace

A good judge of effective training is to perform this workout monthly with the goal to increase distance each session

TOTAL DISTANCE = 3 - 4 MILES

What you need to know for this workout:
Marathon Pace, 5K Pace

Example Female (21:00 5K Goal)   **Example Male (18:00 5K Goal)**

Begin at 7.8 MPH
Goal is to Finish at speed
of 8.9 MPH
Record Total Distance

Begin at 9.1 MPH
Goal is to Finish at speed
of 10.3 MPH
Record Total Distance

Pace Variation

1 Mile at Marathon Pace

.75 Miles at 5K Pace

.5 Miles at Marathon Pace

.5 Miles at 5K Pace

.75 Miles at Marathon Pace

1 Mile at 5K Pace

TOTAL DISTANCE = 4.5 MILES

What you need to know for this workout:
Marathon Pace, 5K Pace

Example Female (22:00 5K Goal)	Example Male (19:00 5K Goal)
0 – 1 Mile = 7.5 MPH	0 – 1 Mile = 8.7 MPH
1 – 1.75 Miles = 8.5 MPH	1 – 1.75 Miles = 9.8 MPH
1.75 – 2.25 Miles = 7.5 MPH	1.75 – 2.25 Miles = 8.7 MPH
2.25 – 2.75 Miles = 8.5 MPH	2.25 – 2.75 Miles = 9.8 MPH
2.75 – 3.5 Miles = 7.5 MPH	2.75 – 3.5 Miles = 8.7 MPH
3.5 – 4.5 Miles = 8.5 MPH	3.5 – 4.5 Miles = 9.8 MPH

400's with Short Recovery

400 at 5K pace

Recovery .1 Miles

Repeat sequence 9 additional times (10 sequences total)

TOTAL DISTANCE = 3.4 MILES (including recovery)

What you need to know for this workout:
5K Pace

Example Female (21:30 5K Goal)	Example Male (18:30 5K Goal)
0 - .25 Miles = 8.7 MPH	0 - .25 Miles = 10.1 MPH
.25 - .35 Miles = Recovery	.25 - .35 Miles = Recovery
.35 - .6 Miles = 8.7 MPH	.35 - .6 Miles = 10.1 MPH
.6 - .7 Miles = Recovery	.6 - .7 Miles = Recovery
.7 - .95 Miles = 8.7 MPH	.7 - .95 Miles = 10.1 MPH
.95 – 1.05 Miles = Recovery	.95 – 1.05 Miles = Recovery
1.05 – 1.3 Miles = 8.7 MPH	1.05 – 1.3 Miles = 10.1 MPH
1.3 – 1.4 Miles = Recovery	1.3 – 1.4 Miles = Recovery
1.4 – 1.65 Miles = 8.7 MPH	1.4 – 1.65 Miles = 10.1 MPH
1.65 – 1.75 Miles = Recovery	1.65 – 1.75 Miles = Recovery
1.75 – 2.0 Miles = 8.7 MPH	1.75 – 2.0 Miles = 10.1 MPH
2.0 – 2.1 Miles = Recovery	2.0 – 2.1 Miles = Recovery
2.1 – 2.35 Miles = 8.7 MPH	2.1 – 2.35 Miles = 10.1 MPH
2.35 – 2.45 Miles = Recovery	2.35 – 2.45 Miles = Recovery
2.45 – 2.7 Miles = 8.7 MPH	2.45 – 2.7 Miles = 10.1 MPH
2.7 – 2.8 Miles = Recovery	2.7 – 2.8 Miles = Recovery
2.8 – 3.05 Miles = 8.7 MPH	2.8 – 3.05 Miles = 10.1 MPH
3.05 – 3.15 Miles = Recovery	3.05 – 3.15 Miles = Recovery
3.15 – 3.4 Miles = 8.7 MPH	3.15 – 3.4 Miles = 10.1 MPH

30 / 30 / 60

:30 Seconds at 800 pace

:30 Seconds at 5k pace

:60 Seconds at Marathon Pace

Repeat sequence 14 additional times (15 sequences total)

TOTAL DISTANCE = 3.75 - 5.5 MILES

What you need to know for this workout:
Marathon Pace, 5K Pace, 800 Pace

Example Female (22:30 5K Goal)   **Example Male (17:30 5K Goal)**

0 – 30 Seconds = 9.1 MPH   0 – 30 Seconds = 11.7 MPH
30 – 1 Minute = 8.3 MPH   30 – 1 Minute = 10.6 MPH
1 – 2 Minutes = 7.3 MPH   1 – 2 Minutes = 9.4 MPH
Repeat * 15   Repeat * 15

10 * 1 Minute

:45 Seconds at 5K pace

:15 Seconds recovery

Repeat sequence 9 additional times (10 sequences total)

TOTAL DISTANCE = 1.25 - 1.75 MILES

What you need to know for this workout:
5K Pace

Example Female (20:00 5K Goal)	Example Male (19:30 5K Goal)
0 – 45 Seconds = 9.3 MPH	0 – 45 Seconds = 9.5 MPH
45 – 1 Minute = Recovery	45 – 1 Minute = Recovery
1 – 1:45 Minutes = 9.3 MPH	1 – 1:45 Minutes = 9.5 MPH
1:45 – 2:00 Minutes = Recovery	1:45 – 2:00 Minutes = Recovery
2:00 – 2:45 Minutes = 9.3 MPH	2:00 – 2:45 Minutes = 9.5 MPH
2:45 – 3:00 Minutes = Recovery	2:45 – 3:00 Minutes = Recovery
3:00 – 3:45 Minutes = 9.3 MPH	3:00 – 3:45 Minutes = 9.5 MPH
3:45 – 4:00 Minutes = Recovery	3:45 – 4:00 Minutes = Recovery
4:00 – 4:45 Minutes = 9.3 MPH	4:00 – 4:45 Minutes = 9.5 MPH
4:45 – 5:00 Minutes = Recovery	4:45 – 5:00 Minutes = Recovery
5:00 – 5:45 Minutes = 9.3 MPH	5:00 – 5:45 Minutes = 9.5 MPH
5:45 – 6:00 Minutes = Recovery	5:45 – 6:00 Minutes = Recovery
6:00 – 6:45 Minutes = 9.3 MPH	6:00 – 6:45 Minutes = 9.5 MPH
6:45 – 7:00 Minutes = Recovery	6:45 – 7:00 Minutes = Recovery
7:00 – 7:45 Minutes = 9.3 MPH	7:00 – 7:45 Minutes = 9.5 MPH
7:45 – 8:00 Minutes = Recovery	7:45 – 8:00 Minutes = Recovery
8:00 – 8:45 Minutes = 9.3 MPH	8:00 – 8:45 Minutes = 9.5 MPH
8:45 – 9:00 Minutes = Recovery	8:45 – 9:00 Minutes = Recovery
9:00 – 9:45 Minutes = 9.3 MPH	9:00 – 9:45 Minutes = 9.5 MPH

3 * (1, 2, 3)

1 Minute at 5K Pace

2 Minutes at Marathon Pace

3 Minutes at 5k Pace

Recover :90 seconds

Repeat Sequence 2 additional times (3 sequences total)

TOTAL DISTANCE = 2.75 - 3.75 MILES

What you need to know for this workout:
Marathon Pace, 5K Pace

Example Female (18:00 5K Goal)

0 – 1 Minute = 10.3 MPH
1 – 3 Minutes = 9.1 MPH
3 – 6 Minutes = 10.3 MPH
6 – 7:30 Minutes = Recovery
7:30 – 8:30 Minutes = 10.3 MPH
8:30 – 10:30 Minutes = 9.1 MPH
10:30 – 13:30 Minutes = 10.3 MPH
13:30 – 15 Minutes = Recovery
15 – 16 Minutes = 10.3 MPH
16 – 18 Minutes = 9.1 MPH
18 – 21 Minutes = 10.3 MPH

Example Male (20:00 5K Goal)

0 – 1 Minute = 9.2 MPH
1 – 3 Minutes = 8.2 MPH
3 – 6 Minutes = 9.2 MPH
6 – 7:30 Minutes = Recovery
7:30 – 8:30 Minutes = 9.2 MPH
8:30 – 10:30 Minutes = 8.2 MPH
10:30 – 13:30 Minutes = 9.2 MPH
13:30 – 15 Minutes = Recovery
15 – 16 Minutes = 9.2 MPH
16 – 18 Minutes =8.2 MPH
18 – 21 Minutes = 9.2 MPH

Race Ready

1.0 Mile at Marathon Pace

.75 Miles at Threshold Pace

.75 Miles at 10k pace

.5 Miles at 5k pace

.1 Mile at 800 pace

TOTAL DISTANCE = 3.1 MILES

What you need to know for this workout:
Marathon Pace, Threshold Pace, 10K Pace, 5K Pace, 800 Pace

Example Female (19:00 5K Goal)	Example Male (17:00 5K Goal)
0 – 1 Mile = 8.7 MPH	0 – 1 Mile = 9.7 MPH
1 – 1.75 Miles = 9.2 MPH	1 – 1.75 Miles = 10.2 MPH
1.75 – 2.5 Miles = 9.5 MPH	1.75 – 2.5 Miles = 10.6 MPH
2.5 – 3.0 Miles = 9.8 MPH	2.5 – 3.0 Miles = 11.0 MPH
3.0 – 3.1 Miles = 10.7 MPH	3.0 – 3.1 Miles = 12.0 MPH

Fast Day

1 Mile starting at 10K Pace

Increasing .1 MPH every .1 Mile

Recovery 3 – 4 minutes

Repeat 2 additional sequences (3 sequences total)

TOTAL DISTANCE = 3 MILES

What you need to know for this workout:
10K Pace

Example Female (20:30 5K Goal)

0 - .1 Mile = 8.8 MPH
.1 - .2 Mile = 8.9 MPH
.2 - .3 Mile = 9.0 MPH
.3 - .4 Mile = 9.1 MPH
.4 - .5 Mile = 9.2 MPH
.5 - .6 Mile = 9.3 MPH
.6 - .7 Mile = 9.4 MPH
.7 - .8 Mile = 9.5 MPH
.8 - .9 Mile = 9.6 MPH
.9 – 1.0 Mile = 9.7 MPH
Recover 3 Minutes
Repeat

Example Male (16:00 5K Goal)

0 - .1 Mile = 11.2 MPH
.1 - .2 Mile = 11.3 MPH
.2 - .3 Mile = 11.4 MPH
.3 - .4 Mile = 11.5 MPH
.4 - .5 Mile = 11.6 MPH
.5 - .6 Mile = 11.7 MPH
.6 - .7 Mile = 11.8 MPH
.7 - .8 Mile = 11.9 MPH
.8 - .9 Mile = 12.0 MPH
.9 – 1.0 Mile = 12.1 MPH
Recover 3 Minutes
Repeat

Long Day

15 Minutes at Marathon Pace

15 Minutes at Threshold Pace

15 Minutes at Marathon Pace

10 Minutes at 10K pace

10 Minutes at Marathon Pace

5 Minutes at 5K pace

TOTAL DISTANCE = 8.5 - 11 MILES

What you need to know for this workout:
Marathon Pace, Threshold Pace, 10K Pace, 5K Pace

Example Female (18:30 5K Goal)   **Example Male (15:30 5K Goal)**

Example Female (18:30 5K Goal)	Example Male (15:30 5K Goal)
0 – 15 Minutes = 8.9 MPH	0 – 15 Minutes = 10.6 MPH
15 – 30 Minutes = 9.4 MPH	15 – 30 Minutes = 11.1 MPH
30 – 45 Minutes = 8.9 MPH	30 – 45 Minutes = 10.6 MPH
45 – 55 Minutes = 9.7 MPH	45 – 55 Minutes = 11.6 MPH
55 – 65 Minutes = 8.9 MPH	55 – 65 Minutes = 10.6 MPH
65 – 70 Minutes = 10.1 MPH	65 – 70 Minutes = 12.0 MPH

Threshold Pace

10 Minutes at Marathon Pace

20 Minutes at Threshold Pace

10 Minutes at Marathon Pace

15 Minutes at Threshold Pace

5 Minutes at Marathon Pace

10 Minutes at Threshold Pace

TOTAL DISTANCE = 9 - 12 MILES

What you need to know for this workout:
Marathon Pace, Threshold Pace

Example Female (19:30 5K Goal)	Example Male (17:00 5K Goal)
0 – 10 Minutes = 8.4 MPH	0 – 10 Minutes = 9.7 MPH
10 – 30 Minutes = 9.0 MPH	10 – 30 Minutes = 10.2 MPH
30 – 40 Minutes = 8.4 MPH	30 – 40 Minutes = 9.7 MPH
40 – 55 Minutes = 9.0 MPH	40 – 55 Minutes = 10.2 MPH
55 – 60 Minutes = 8.4 MPH	55 – 60 Minutes = 9.7 MPH
60 – 70 Minutes = 9.0 MPH	60 – 70 Minutes = 10.2 MPH

~

Advanced
½ Marathon Workouts

~

Advanced ½ Marathon

Female: training for a ½ Marathon with a personal best ½ Marathon time below 1 hour and 45 minutes

Male: training for a ½ Marathon with a personal best ½ Marathon time below 1 hour and 30 minutes

The workouts in this section are designed for ½ Marathon runners with a personal best time below 1:45 for females, and below 1:30 minutes for males.

Before each workout it is strongly recommended to do a warm up. After each workout it is highly advisable to perform cool down activities.

Each workout provides sample treadmill running paces based on your ½ Marathon goal pace. Additional ½ Marathon goal times and respective paces can be found in the charts section (located at the end of this book).

"There is no telling how many miles you have to run while chasing a dream. "

20 * 400

1st – 10th 400 (.25 miles) with .05 Mile break between 400's

11th – 15th 400 (.25 miles) with .1 Mile break between 400's

16th – 20th 400 (.25 miles) with .15 Mile break between 400's

Start at Marathon Pace then increase .1 MPH in speed each 400 (.25 miles)

TOTAL DISTANCE = 5 MILES

What you need to know for this workout:
Marathon Pace

Example Female (1:45 13.1 Goal)   Example Male (1:25 13.1 Goal)

Example Female (1:45 13.1 Goal)	Example Male (1:25 13.1 Goal)
0 - .25 Miles = 7.2 MPH	0 - .25 Miles = 8.9 MPH
.25 - .30 Miles = Rest	.25 - .30 Miles = Rest
.30 - .55 Miles = 7.3 MPH	.30 - .55 Miles = 9.0 MPH
.55 - .60 Miles = Rest	.55 - .60 Miles = Rest
.60 - .85 Miles = 7.4 MPH	.60 - .85 Miles = 9.1 MPH
.85 - .90 Miles = Rest	.85 - .90 Miles = Rest
.90 – 1.15 Miles = 7.5 MPH	.90 – 1.15 Miles = 9.2 MPH
1.15 – 1.20 Miles = Rest	1.15 – 1.20 Miles = Rest
1.20 – 1.45 Miles = 7.6 MPH	1.20 – 1.45 Miles = 9.3 MPH
1.45 – 1.50 Miles = Rest	1.45 – 1.50 Miles = Rest
1.50 – 1.75 Miles = 7.7 MPH	1.50 – 1.75 Miles = 9.4 MPH
1.75 – 1.80 Miles = Rest	1.75 – 1.80 Miles = Rest
1.80 – 2.05 Miles = 7.8 MPH	1.80 – 2.05 Miles = 9.5 MPH
2.05 – 2.10 Miles = Rest	2.05 – 2.10 Miles = Rest
2.10 – 2.35 Miles = 7.9 MPH	2.10 – 2.35 Miles = 9.6 MPH
2.35 – 2.40 Miles = Rest	2.35 – 2.40 Miles = Rest
2.40 – 2.65 Miles = 8.0 MPH	2.40 – 2.65 Miles = 9.7 MPH
2.65 – 2.70 Miles = Rest	2.65 – 2.70 Miles = Rest
2.70 – 2.95 Miles = 8.1 MPH	2.70 – 2.95 Miles = 9.8 MPH
2.95 – 3.00 Miles = Rest	2.95 – 3.00 Miles = Rest
3.00 – 3.25 Miles = 8.2 MPH	3.00 – 3.25 Miles = 9.9 MPH
3.25 – 3.35 Miles = Rest	3.25 – 3.35 Miles = Rest
3.35 – 3.60 Miles = 8.3 MPH	3.35 – 3.60 Miles = 10.0 MPH
3.60 – 3.70 Miles = Rest	3.60 – 3.70 Miles = Rest
3.70 – 3.95 Miles = 8.4 MPH	3.70 – 3.95 Miles = 10.1 MPH
3.95 – 4.05 Miles = Rest	3.95 – 4.05 Miles = Rest
4.05 – 4.30 Miles = 8.5 MPH	4.05 – 4.30 Miles = 10.2 MPH
4.30 – 4.40 Miles = Rest	4.30 – 4.40 Miles = Rest
4.40 – 4.65 Miles = 8.6 MPH	4.40 – 4.65 Miles = 10.3 MPH
4.65 – 4.75 Miles = Rest	4.65 – 4.75 Miles = Rest
4.75 – 5.0 Miles = 8.7 MPH	4.75 – 5.0 Miles = 10.4 MPH
5.0 – 5.15 Miles = Rest	5.0 – 5.15 Miles = Rest
5.15 – 5.40 Miles = 8.8 MPH	5.15 – 5.40 Miles = 10.5 MPH
5.40 – 5.55 Miles = Rest	5.40 – 5.55 Miles = Rest
5.55 – 5.80 Miles = 8.9 MPH	5.55 – 5.80 Miles = 10.6 MPH
5.80 – 5.95 Miles = Rest	5.80 – 5.95 Miles = Rest
5.95 – 6.20 Miles = 9.0 MPH	5.95 – 6.20 Miles = 10.7 MPH
6.20 – 6.35 Miles = Rest	6.20 – 6.35 Miles = Rest
6:35 – 6.60 Miles = 9.1 MPH	6:35 – 6.60 Miles = 10.8 MPH

Meet in the Middle

Start at .5 MPH slower than Marathon Pace

After 2 minutes, increase to 1600 pace for 1 minute

Increase slower speed .1 MPH after each 2 Minutes

Decrease faster speed .1 MPH after each 1 Minute

Workout ends once you reach the same speed on both the faster and slower speed

TOTAL DISTANCE = 4 - 6 MILES

What you need to know for this workout:
Marathon Pace, 1600 Pace

Example Female (1:30 13.1 Goal)   Example Male (1:20 13.1 Goal)

0 – 2 Minutes = 7.9 MPH	0 – 2 Minutes = 8.9 MPH
2 – 3 Minutes = 10.1 MPH	2 – 3 Minutes = 11.3 MPH
3 – 5 Minutes = 8.0 MPH	3 – 5 Minutes = 9.0 MPH
5 – 6 Minutes = 10.0 MPH	5 – 6 Minutes = 11.2 MPH
6 – 8 Minutes = 8.1 MPH	6 – 8 Minutes = 9.1 MPH
8 – 9 Minutes = 9.9 MPH	8 – 9 Minutes = 11.1 MPH
9 – 11 Minutes = 8.2 MPH	9 – 11 Minutes = 9.2 MPH
11 – 12 Minutes = 9.8 MPH	11 – 12 Minutes = 11.0 MPH
12 – 14 Minutes = 8.3 MPH	12 – 14 Minutes = 9.3 MPH
14 – 15 Minutes = 9.7 MPH	14 – 15 Minutes = 10.9 MPH
15 – 17 Minutes = 8.4 MPH	15 – 17 Minutes = 9.4 MPH
17 – 18 Minutes = 9.6 MPH	17 – 18 Minutes = 10.8 MPH
18 – 20 Minutes = 8.5 MPH	18 – 20 Minutes = 9.5 MPH
20 – 21 Minutes = 9.5 MPH	20 – 21 Minutes = 10.7 MPH
21 – 23 Minutes = 8.6 MPH	21 – 23 Minutes = 9.6 MPH
23 – 24 Minutes = 9.4 MPH	23 – 24 Minutes = 10.6 MPH
24 – 26 Minutes = 8.7 MPH	24 – 26 Minutes = 9.7 MPH
26 – 27 Minutes = 9.3 MPH	26 – 27 Minutes = 10.5 MPH
27 – 29 Minutes = 8.8 MPH	27 – 29 Minutes = 9.8 MPH
29 – 30 Minutes = 9.2 MPH	29 – 30 Minutes = 10.4 MPH
30 – 32 Minutes = 8.9 MPH	30 – 32 Minutes = 9.9 MPH
32 – 33 Minutes = 9.1 MPH	32 – 33 Minutes = 10.3 MPH
33- 35 Minutes = 9.0 MPH	33- 35 Minutes = 10.0 MPH
	35 – 36 Minutes = 10.2 MPH
	36 – 38 Minutes = 10.1 MPH

Incline Workout

Start at Marathon Pace

Increase incline every 2 minutes from 0% - 4% and decrease from 4% - 0% accordingly

Recover 3-5 minutes and repeat at .1 MPH faster

TOTAL DISTANCE = 8 - 9 MILES

What you need to know for this workout:
Marathon Pace

Example Female (1:35 13.1 Goal)	**Example Male (1:30 13.1 Goal)**
Pace for Round 1 = 8.0 MPH	Pace for Round 1 = 8.4 MPH
Pace for Round 2 = 8.1 MPH	Pace for Round 2 = 8.5 MPH
Pace for Round 3 = 8.2 MPH	Pace for Round 3 = 8.6 MPH
0 – 2 Minutes = 0% Incline	0 – 2 Minutes = 0% Incline
2 – 4 Minutes = 1% Incline	2 – 4 Minutes = 1% Incline
4 – 6 Minutes = 2% Incline	4 – 6 Minutes = 2% Incline
6 – 8 Minutes = 3% Incline	6 – 8 Minutes = 3% Incline
8 – 10 Minutes = 4% Incline	8 – 10 Minutes = 4% Incline
10 – 12 Minutes = 4% Incline	10 – 12 Minutes = 4% Incline
12 – 14 Minutes = 3% Incline	12 – 14 Minutes = 3% Incline
14 – 16 Minutes = 2% Incline	14 – 16 Minutes = 2% Incline
16 – 18 Minutes = 1% Incline	16 – 18 Minutes = 1% Incline
18 – 20 Minutes = 0% Incline	18 – 20 Minutes = 0% Incline
Recover 3 Minutes	Recover 3 Minutes
Repeat	Repeat

13.1 Simulation

4 Miles at .5 slower than Marathon pace

4 Miles at Marathon Pace

4 Miles at Half Marathon Pace

1.1 Miles at Threshold Pace

TOTAL DISTANCE = 13.1 MILES

What you need to know for this workout:
Marathon Pace, Half Marathon Pace, Threshold Pace

Example Female (1:40 13.1 Goal)	Example Male (1:15 13.1 Goal)
0 – 4 Miles = 7.1 MPH	0 – 4 Miles = 9.6 MPH
4 – 8 Miles = 7.6 MPH	4 – 8 Miles = 10.1 MPH
8 – 12 Miles = 7.9 MPH	8 – 12 Miles = 10.5 MPH
12 – 13.1 Miles = 8.1 MPH	12 – 13.1 Miles = 10.6 MPH

800 Meter Repeats

10 * 800 (.5 miles) starting at 10k pace and increasing .1 MPH each 800

Active Rest .25 miles between 800's (50% of pace)

TOTAL DISTANCE = 7.25 MILES

What you need to know for this workout:
10K Pace

Example Female (1:40 13.1 Goal)	Example Male (1:25 13.1 Goal)
0 - .5 Miles = 8.3 MPH	0 - .5 Miles = 9.7 MPH
.5 - .75 Miles = 4.1 MPH rest	.5 - .75 Miles = 4.8 MPH rest
.75 – 1.25 Miles = 8.4 MPH	.75 – 1.25 Miles = 9.8 MPH
1.25 – 1.5 Miles = 4.2 MPH rest	1.25 – 1.5 Miles = 4.9 MPH rest
1.5 – 2.0 Miles = 8.5 MPH	1.5 – 2.0 Miles = 9.9 MPH
2.0 – 2.25 Miles = 4.3 MPH rest	2.0 – 2.25 Miles = 4.9 MPH rest
2.25 – 2.75 Miles = 8.6 MPH	2.25 – 2.75 Miles = 10.0 MPH
2.75 – 3.0 Miles = 4.3 MPH rest	2.75 – 3.0 Miles = 5.0 MPH rest
3.0 – 3.5 Miles = 8.7 MPH	3.0 – 3.5 Miles = 10.1 MPH
3.5 – 3.75 Miles = 4.4 MPH rest	3.5 – 3.75 Miles = 5.0 MPH rest
3.75 – 4.25 Miles = 8.8 MPH	3.75 – 4.25 Miles = 10.2 MPH
4.25 – 4.5 Miles = 4.4 MPH rest	4.25 – 4.5 Miles = 5.1 MPH rest
4.5 – 5.0 Miles = 8.9 MPH	4.5 – 5.0 Miles = 10.3 MPH
5.0 – 5.25 Miles = 4.5 MPH rest	5.0 – 5.25 Miles = 5.1 MPH rest
5.25 – 5.75 Miles = 9.0 MPH	5.25 – 5.75 Miles = 10.4 MPH
5.75 – 6.0 Miles = 4.5 MPH rest	5.75 – 6.0 Miles = 5.2 MPH rest
6.0 – 6.5 Miles = 9.1 MPH	6.0 – 6.5 Miles = 10.5 MPH
6.5 – 6.75 Miles = 4.6 MPH rest	6.5 – 6.75 Miles = 5.2 MPH rest
6.75 – 7.25 Miles = 9.2 MPH	6.75 – 7.25 Miles = 10.6 MPH

Pace Time

10 Minutes .5 MPH slower than Marathon Pace

10 Minutes Marathon Pace

10 Minutes Half Marathon Pace

10 Minutes Threshold Pace

5 Minutes 10K pace

5 Minutes 5k Pace

TOTAL DISTANCE = 7 - 9 MILES

What you need to know for this workout:
Marathon Pace, Half Marathon Pace, Threshold Pace, 10K Pace,
5K Pace

Example Female (1:30 13.1 Goal)	Example Male (1:20 13.1 Goal)
0 – 10 Minutes =7.9 MPH	0 – 10 Minutes =8.9 MPH
10 – 20 Minutes = 8.4 MPH	10 – 20 Minutes = 9.4 MPH
20 – 30 Minutes = 8.7 MPH	20 – 30 Minutes = 9.8 MPH
30 – 40 Minutes = 8.9 MPH	30 – 40 Minutes = 9.9 MPH
40 – 45 Minutes = 9.2 MPH	40 – 45 Minutes = 10.3 MPH
45 – 50 Minutes = 9.5 MPH	45 – 50 Minutes = 10.7 MPH

30 Minute Time Trial

Start at Marathon Pace and increase .1 MPH each minute until Time Trial pace has been achieved

Hold Time Trial pace for the remainder of the 30 minutes

Record Distance

Workout can be done monthly as a fitness assessment

Individual is in charge of determining Time Trial Pace

TOTAL DISTANCE = 4 - 6 MILES

What you need to know for this workout:
Marathon Pace

Example Female (1:25 13.1 Goal)	Example Male (1:10 13.1 Goal)
0 – 1 Minute = 8.9 MPH	0 – 1 Minute = 10.7 MPH
Continue to increase .1 MPH	Continue to increase .1 MPH
Until Time Trail Pace Achieved	Until Time Trail Pace Achieved
(Pace determined by individual)	(Pace determined by individual)
CAUTION – Overestimating	CAUTION – Overestimating
Time Trial Pace May Result in	Time Trial Pace May Result in
The inability to complete 30 mins.	The inability to complete 30 mins.

Long Run Test

60 Minutes at .5 MPH slower than Marathon Pace

10 Minutes at Marathon Pace

20 Minutes at Half Marathon Pace

10 Minutes at Threshold Pace

TOTAL DISTANCE = 12 - 15 MILES

What you need to know for this workout:
Marathon Pace, Half Marathon Pace, Threshold Pace

Example Female (1:45 13.1 Goal)	Example Male (1:20 13.1 Goal)
0 – 60 Minutes = 6.7 MPH	0 – 60 Minutes = 8.9 MPH
This should feel comfortable and conversational, if not, decrease pace until desired comfort is reached	*This should feel comfortable and conversational, if not, decrease pace until desired comfort is reached*
60 – 70 Minutes = 7.2 MPH	60 – 70 Minutes = 9.4 MPH
70 – 90 Minutes = 7.5 MPH	70 – 90 Minutes = 9.8 MPH
90 – 100 Minutes = 7.7 MPH	90 – 100 Minutes = 9.9 MPH

Switching Gears

1 Mile at Threshold Pace

1 Mile at 10K Pace

1 Mile at Marathon Pace

1 Mile at Threshold Pace

1 Mile at Half Marathon Pace

1 Mile at Marathon Pace

1 Mile at Threshold Pace

1 Mile at 5k Pace

1 Mile at Half Marathon Pace

TOTAL DISTANCE = 9 MILES

What you need to know for this workout:
Marathon Pace, Half Marathon Pace, Threshold Pace, 10K Pace,
5K Pace

Example Female (1:35 13.1 Goal)	Example Male (1:25 13.1 Goal)
0 – 1 Mile = 8.5 MPH	0 – 1 Mile = 9.4 MPH
1 – 2 Miles = 8.7 MPH	1 – 2 Miles = 9.7 MPH
2 – 3 Miles = 8.0 MPH	2 – 3 Miles = 8.9 MPH
3 – 4 Miles = 8.5 MPH	3 – 4 Miles = 9.4 MPH
4 – 5 Miles = 8.3 MPH	4 – 5 Miles = 9.3 MPH
5 – 6 Miles = 8.0 MPH	5 – 6 Miles = 8.9 MPH
6 – 7 Miles = 8.5 MPH	6 – 7 Miles = 9.4 MPH
7 – 8 Miles = 9.0 MPH	7 – 8 Miles = 10.1 MPH
8 – 9 Miles = 8.3 MPH	8 – 9 Miles = 9.3 MPH

Race Pace

6 * 1 Mile at Half Marathon Pace

.25 Miles Recovery at Marathon Pace after each Mile

TOTAL DISTANCE = 7.5 MILES

What you need to know for this workout:
Marathon Pace, Half Marathon Pace

Example Female (1:15 13.1 Goal)	Example Male (1:20 13.1 Goal)
0 – 1 Mile = 10.5 MPH	0 – 1 Mile = 9.8 MPH
1 – 1.25 Miles = 10.1 MPH	1 – 1.25 Miles = 9.4 MPH
1.25 – 2.25 Miles = 10.5 MPH	1.25 – 2.25 Miles = 9.8 MPH
2.25 – 2.5 Miles = 10.1 MPH	2.25 – 2.5 Miles = 9.4 MPH
2.5 – 3.5 Miles = 10.5 MPH	2.5 – 3.5 Miles = 9.8 MPH
3.5 – 3.75 Miles = 10.1 MPH	3.5 – 3.75 Miles = 9.4 MPH
3.75 – 4.75 Miles = 10.5 MPH	3.75 – 4.75 Miles = 9.8 MPH
4.75 – 5.0 Miles = 10.1 MPH	4.75 – 5.0 Miles = 9.4 MPH
5.0 – 6.0 Miles = 10.5 MPH	5.0 – 6.0 Miles = 9.8 MPH
6.0 – 6.25 Miles = 10.1 MPH	6.0 – 6.25 Miles = 9.4 MPH
6.25 – 7.25 Miles = 10.5 MPH	6.25 – 7.25 Miles = 9.8 MPH
7.25 – 7.5 Miles = 10.1 MPH	7.25 – 7.5 Miles = 9.4 MPH

~

Advanced
Marathon Workouts

~

Advanced Marathon

Female: training for a Marathon with a personal best Marathon time below 3 hours and 25 minutes

Male: training for a Marathon with a personal best Marathon time below 3 hours

The workouts in this section are designed for Marathon runners with a personal best time below 3:25 for females, and 3:00 for males.

Before each workout it is strongly recommended to do a warm up. After each workout it is highly advisable to perform cool down activities.

Each workout provides sample treadmill running paces based on your Marathon goal pace. Additional Marathon goal times and respective paces can be found in the charts section (located at the end of this book).

"The ability to run the extra mile lies between your ears. "

90 Minute Run

Start at 95% Marathon Pace

Increase .1 MPH every 15 minutes for 90 Minutes

TOTAL DISTANCE = 11.5 - 15 MILES

What you need to know for this workout:
95% Marathon Pace

Example Female (2:45 26.2 Goal)   **Example Male (2:25 26.2 Goal)**

Example Female (2:45 26.2 Goal)	Example Male (2:25 26.2 Goal)
0 – 15 Minutes = 9.0 MPH	0 – 15 Minutes = 10.3 MPH
15 – 30 Minutes = 9.1 MPH	15 – 30 Minutes = 10.4 MPH
30 – 45 Minutes = 9.2 MPH	30 – 45 Minutes = 10.5 MPH
45 – 60 Minutes = 9.3 MPH	45 – 60 Minutes = 10.6 MPH
60 – 75 Minutes = 9.4 MPH	60 – 75 Minutes = 10.7 MPH
75 – 90 Minutes = 9.5 MPH	75 – 90 Minutes = 10.8 MPH

13 Mile Grind

2 Miles at 80% Marathon Pace

2 Miles at 85% Marathon Pace

2 Miles at 90% Marathon Pace

2 Miles at 95% Marathon Pace

2 Miles at Marathon Pace

2 Miles at 105% Marathon Pace

1 Mile at 110% Marathon Pace

TOTAL DISTANCE = 13 MILES

What you need to know for this workout:
80% Marathon Pace, 85% Marathon Pace, 90% Marathon Pace,
95% Marathon Pace, 100% Marathon Pace, 105% Marathon
Pace, 110% Marathon Pace

Example Female (3:20 26.2 Goal)	Example Male (2:30 26.2 Goal)
0 – 2 Miles: 6.6 MPH	0 – 2 Miles: 8.7 MPH
2 – 4 Miles: 6.8 MPH	2 – 4 Miles: 9.1 MPH
4 – 6 Miles: 7.1 MPH	4 – 6 Miles: 9.5 MPH
6 – 8 Miles: 7.5 MPH	6 – 8 Miles: 10.0 MPH
8 – 10 Miles: 7.9 MPH	8 – 10 Miles: 10.5 MPH
10 – 12 Miles: 8.3 MPH	10 – 12 Miles: 11.0 MPH
12 – 13 Miles: 8.7 MPH	12 – 13 Miles: 11.6 MPH

60 Minutes * 2

1st 60 minutes start at 70% Marathon Pace and increase throughout run to 80% Marathon Pace

Hydrate & Refuel for 30 seconds – 3 minutes.

2nd 60 minutes start at 80% Marathon Pace and increase .1 MPH every 3 minutes.

TOTAL DISTANCE = 13 MILES

What you need to know for this workout:
70% Marathon Pace, 80% Marathon Pace

Example Female (3:00 26.2 Goal)	Example Male (2:50 26.2 Goal)
0 – 60 Minutes = 6.7 – 7.3 MPH	0 – 60 Minutes = 7.1 – 7.7 MPH
60 – 63 Minutes = 7.3 MPH	60 – 63 Minutes = 7.7 MPH
63 – 66 Minutes = 7.4 MPH	63 – 66 Minutes = 7.8 MPH
66 – 69 Minutes = 7.5 MPH	66 – 69 Minutes = 7.9 MPH
69 – 72 Minutes = 7.6 MPH	69 – 72 Minutes = 8.0 MPH
72 – 75 Minutes = 7.7 MPH	72 – 75 Minutes = 8.1 MPH
75 – 78 Minutes = 7.8 MPH	75 – 78 Minutes = 8.2 MPH
78 – 81 Minutes = 7.9 MPH	78 – 81 Minutes = 8.3 MPH
81 – 84 Minutes = 8.0 MPH	81 – 84 Minutes = 8.4 MPH
84 – 87 Minutes = 8.1 MPH	84 – 87 Minutes = 8.5 MPH
87 – 90 Minutes = 8.2 MPH	87 – 90 Minutes = 8.6 MPH
90 – 93 Minutes = 8.3 MPH	90 – 93 Minutes = 8.7 MPH
93 – 96 Minutes = 8.4 MPH	93 – 96 Minutes = 8.8 MPH
96 – 99 Minutes = 8.5 MPH	96 – 99 Minutes = 8.9 MPH
99 – 102 Minutes = 8.6 MPH	99 – 102 Minutes = 9.0 MPH
102 – 105 Minutes = 8.7 MPH	102 – 105 Minutes = 9.1 MPH
105 – 108 Minutes = 8.8 MPH	105 – 108 Minutes = 9.2 MPH
108 – 111 Minutes = 8.9 MPH	108 – 111 Minutes = 9.3 MPH
111 – 114 Minutes = 9.0 MPH	111 – 114 Minutes = 9.4 MPH
114 – 117 Minutes = 9.1 MPH	114 – 117 Minutes = 9.5 MPH
117 – 120 Minutes = 9.2 MPH	117 – 120 Minutes = 9.6 MPH

Steady Marathon

15 Minute at Marathon Pace

30 Minute at 110% Marathon Pace

15 Minute at Marathon Pace

15 Minute at 110% Marathon Pace

TOTAL DISTANCE = 9 - 11 MILES

What you need to know for this workout:
100% Marathon Pace, 110% Marathon Pace

Example Female (3:15 26.2 Goal)

1 – 15 Minutes = 8.1 MPH
15 – 45 Minutes = 8.9 MPH
45 – 60 Minutes = 8.1 MPH
60 – 75 Minutes = 8.9 MPH

Example Male (2:55 26.2 Goal)

1 – 15 Minutes = 9.0 MPH
15 – 45 Minutes = 10.0 MPH
45 – 60 Minutes = 9.0 MPH
60 – 75 Minutes = 10.0 MPH

Yasso 800's

10 * 800 (.5 miles) repeats at goal marathon time (i.e. 3:00 hour marathon goal = 3:00 minute 800) with 400 (.25 miles) jog in between repeats

This can get confusing especially as you fatigue as you get higher in repeats. A suggestion is to write the following and tape to your treadmill:

Complete Repeat 1 - .5 Miles
Complete Jog 1 - .75 Miles
Complete Repeat 2 – 1.25 Miles
Complete Jog 2 – 1.5 Miles
Complete Repeat 3 – 2.0 Miles
Complete Jog 3 – 2.25 Miles
Complete Repeat 4 – 2.75 Miles
Complete Jog 4 – 3.0 Miles
Complete Repeat 5 – 3.5 Miles
Complete Jog 5 – 3.75 Miles
Complete Repeat 6 – 4.25 Miles
Complete Jog 6 – 4.5 Miles
Complete Repeat 7 – 5.0 Miles
Complete Jog 7 – 5.25 Miles
Complete Repeat 8 – 5.75 Miles
Complete Jog 8 – 6.0 Miles
Complete Repeat 9 – 6.5 Miles
Complete Jog 9 – 6.75 Miles
Complete Repeat 10 – 7.25 Miles
Complete Jog 10 – 7.5 Miles

TOTAL DISTANCE = 7.5 MILES

What you need to know for this workout:
100% Marathon Pace

Example Female (2:45 26.2 Goal)   **Example Male (2:25 26.2 Goal)**

Repeats = 9.5 MPH   Repeats = 10.8 MPH
Recovery = 4.8 MPH   Recovery = 5.4 MPH

Pyramid Workout

2 sets of the following:

400 (.25 Miles) at 120% Marathon Pace

800 (.5 Miles) at 115% Marathon Pace

3200 (2 Miles) at Marathon Pace

800 (.5 Miles) at 115% Marathon Pace

400 (.25 Miles) at 120% Marathon Pace

No recovery between repetitions

5 minute active recovery between Sequences (2 total sequences)

TOTAL DISTANCE = 6.5 MILES

What you need to know for this workout:
100% Marathon Pace, 115% Marathon Pace, 120% Marathon
Pace

Example Female (3:00 26.2 Goal)	Example Male (2:45 26.2 Goal)
.00 - .25 Miles = 10.9 MPH	.00 - .25 Miles = 11.9 MPH
.25 - .5 Miles = 10.2 MPH	.25 - .5 Miles = 11.2 MPH
.5 – 2.5 Miles = 8.7 MPH	.5 – 2.5 Miles = 9.5 MPH
2.5 – 3.0 Miles = 10.2 MPH	2.5 – 3.0 Miles = 11.2 MPH
3.0 – 3.25 Miles = 10.9 MPH	3.0 – 3.25 Miles = 11.9 MPH
Recover 5 Minutes	Recover 5 Minutes
Repeat	Repeat

Split Workout

4 Miles at Marathon Pace

3 * 400 (.25 miles) 1st 400 at 110% Marathon Pace, 2nd 400 at 80% Marathon Pace, 3rd 400 at 110% Marathon Pace

3 Miles at Marathon Pace

3 * 400 (.25 miles) 1st 400 at 115% Marathon Pace, 2nd 400 at 80% Marathon Pace, 3rd 400 at 115% Marathon Pace

2 Miles at Marathon Pace

3 * 400 (.25 miles) 1st 400 at 120% Marathon Pace, 2nd 400 at 80% Marathon Pace, 3rd 400 at 120% Marathon Pace

1 Mile at Marathon Pace

2 * 800 at 115% Marathon Pace, 400 (.25 miles) Recovery at 80% Marathon Pace between reps

TOTAL DISTANCE = 14.5 MILES

What you need to know for this workout:
80% Marathon Pace, 85% Marathon Pace, 100% Marathon Pace, 110% Marathon Pace, 115% Marathon Pace, 120% Marathon Pace

Example Female (3:20 26.2 Goal)

.00 – 4.0 Miles = 7.9 MPH
4.0 – 4.25 Miles = 8.7 MPH
4.25 – 4.5 Miles = 6.6 MPH
4.5 – 4.75 Miles = 8.7 MPH
4.75 – 5 Miles = 6.6 MPH
5.0 – 8.0 Miles = 7.9 MPH
8.0 – 8.25 Miles = 9.2 MPH
8.25 – 8.5 Miles = 6.6 MPH
8.5 – 8.75 Miles = 9.2 MPH
8.75 – 9.0 Miles = 6.6 MPH
9.0 – 11.0 Miles = 7.9 MPH
11.0 – 11.25 Miles = 9.8 MPH
11.25 – 11.5 Miles = 6.6 MPH
11.5 – 11.75 Miles = 9.8 MPH
11.75 – 12.0 Miles = 6.6 MPH
12.0 – 13.0 Miles = 7.9 MPH
13.0 – 13.5 Miles = 9.2 MPH
13.5 – 13.75 Miles = 6.6 MPH
13.75 – 14.25 Miles = 9.2 MPH
14.25 – 14.5 Miles = 6.6 MPH

Example Male (2:25 26.2 Goal)

.00 – 4.0 Miles = 10.8 MPH
4.0 – 4.25 Miles = 12.1 MPH
4.25 – 4.5 Miles = 9.0 MPH
4.5 – 4.75 Miles = 12.1 MPH
4.75 – 5 Miles = 9.0 MPH
5.0 – 8.0 Miles = 10.8 MPH
8.0 – 8.25 Miles = 12.7 MPH
8.25 – 8.5 Miles = 9.0 MPH
8.5 – 8.75 Miles = 12.7 MPH
8.75 – 9.0 Miles = 9.0 MPH
9.0 – 11.0 Miles = 10.8 MPH
11.0 – 11.25 Miles = 13.5 MPH
11.25 – 11.5 Miles = 9.0 MPH
11.5 – 11.75 Miles = 13.5 MPH
11.75 – 12.0 Miles = 9.0 MPH
12.0 – 13.0 Miles = 10.8 MPH
13.0 – 13.5 Miles = 12.7 MPH
13.5 – 13.75 Miles = 9.0 MPH
13.75 – 14.25 Miles = 12.7 MPH
14.25 – 14.5 Miles = 9.0 MPH

3 Mile Repeats

800 (.5 Miles) at 120% Marathon Pace

800 (.5 Miles) at Marathon Pace

Continue Sequence for 3 Miles

Repeat for 3 – 4 sequences depending on fitness

Rest 3-5 minutes between sets, passive recovery or active recovery of 60% Marathon Pace depending on fitness

TOTAL DISTANCE = 9 - 12 MILES

What you need to know for this workout:
100% Marathon Pace, 120% Marathon Pace

Example Female (3:10 26.2 Goal)	Example Male (2:55 26.2 Goal)
0 - .5 Miles = 10.3 MPH	0 - .5 Miles = 11.2 MPH
.5 – 1.0 Mile = 8.3 MPH	.5 – 1.0 Mile = 9.0 MPH
1.0 – 1.5 Miles = 10.3 MPH	1.0 – 1.5 Miles = 11.2 MPH
1.5 – 2.0 Miles = 8.3 MPH	1.5 – 2.0 Miles = 9.0 MPH
2.0 – 2.5 Miles = 10.3 MPH	2.0 – 2.5 Miles = 11.2 MPH
2.5 – 3.0 Miles = 8.3 MPH	2.5 – 3.0 Miles = 9.0 MPH
Active Recovery Pace = 5.9 MPH	Active Recovery Pace = 6.4 MPH

Marathon Simulation

1 Mile at 80% Marathon Pace

1 Mile at 85% Marathon Pace

1 Mile at 90% Marathon Pace

8 Miles at Marathon Pace

1 Mile at 105% Marathon Pace

1 Mile at 110% Marathon Pace

TOTAL DISTANCE = 13 MILES

What you need to know for this workout:
80% Marathon Pace, 85% Marathon Pace, 90% Marathon Pace,
100% Marathon Pace, 105% Marathon Pace, 110% Marathon
Pace

Example Female (3:05 26.2 Goal)	Example Male (2:50 26.2 Goal)
0 – 1 Mile = 7.1 MPH	0 – 1 Mile = 7.7 MPH
1 – 2 Miles = 7.4 MPH	1 – 2 Miles = 8.0 MPH
2 – 3 Miles = 7.7 MPH	2 – 3 Miles = 8.4 MPH
3 – 11 Miles = 8.5 MPH	3 – 11 Miles = 9.2 MPH
11 – 12 Miles = 8.9 MPH	11 – 12 Miles = 9.7 MPH
12 – 13 Miles = 9.4 MPH	12 – 13 Miles = 10.3 MPH

Long Run Marathon Pace Repeats

1 Mile at Marathon Pace

1 Mile at 70% Marathon Pace

2 Miles at Marathon Pace

1 Mile at 75% Marathon Pace

3 Miles at Marathon Pace

1 Mile at 80% Marathon Pace

3 Miles at Marathon Pace

1 Mile at 85% Marathon Pace

2 Miles at Marathon Pace

1 Mile at 90% Marathon Pace

1 Mile at Marathon Pace

1 Mile at 95% Marathon Pace

1 Mile at Marathon Pace

TOTAL DISTANCE = 19 MILES

What you need to know for this workout:
70% Marathon Pace, 75% Marathon Pace, 80% Marathon Pace,
85% Marathon Pace, 90% Marathon Pace, 95% Marathon Pace,
100% Marathon Pace

Example Female (3:25 26.2 Goal)   Example Male (2:40 26.2 Goal)

0 – 1.0 Mile = 7.7 MPH	0 – 1.0 Mile = 9.8 MPH
1.0 – 2.0 Miles = 5.9 MPH	1.0 – 2.0 Miles = 7.6 MPH
2.0 – 4.0 Miles = 7.7 MPH	2.0 – 4.0 Miles = 9.8 MPH
4.0 – 5.0 Miles = 6.1 MPH	4.0 – 5.0 Miles = 7.9 MPH
5.0 – 8.0 Miles = 7.7MPH	5.0 – 8.0 Miles = 9.8 MPH
8.0 – 9.0 Miles = 6.4 MPH	8.0 – 9.0 Miles = 8.2 MPH
9.0 – 12.0 Miles = 7.7 MPH	9.0 – 12.0 Miles = 9.8 MPH
12.0 – 13.0 Miles = 6.7 MPH	12.0 – 13.0 Miles = 8.5 MPH
13.0 – 15.0 Miles = 7.7 MPH	13.0 – 15.0 Miles = 9.8MPH
15.0 – 16.0 Miles = 7.0MPH	15.0 – 16.0 Miles = 8.9 MPH
16.0 – 17.0 Miles = 7.7 MPH	16.0 – 17.0 Miles = 9.8 MPH
17.0 – 18.0 Miles = 7.3 MPH	17.0 – 18.0 Miles = 9.4 MPH
18.0 – 19.0 Miles = 7.7 MPH	18.0 – 19.0 Miles = 9.8 MPH

~ Pace Charts ~

5K Pace Chart

	400 pace	800 pace	1600 pace	5000 pace
15:00	13.6	13.3	13	12.4
15:30	13.3	13	12.6	12
16:00	13	12.7	12.3	11.6
16:30	12.6	12.3	11.8	11.3
17:00	12.3	12	11.5	11
17:30	12	11.7	11.2	10.6
18:00	11.7	11.4	11	10.3
18:30	11.2	10.9	10.7	10.1
19:00	11	10.7	10.3	9.8
19:30	10.8	10.5	10.1	9.5
20:00	10.5	10.2	9.7	9.3
20:30	10.3	10	9.5	9.1
21:00	10	9.7	9.3	8.9
21:30	9.7	9.4	9.1	8.7
22:00	9.6	9.3	8.9	8.5
22:30	9.4	9.1	8.7	8.3
23:00	9.1	8.8	8.5	8.1
23:30	8.9	8.6	8.3	7.9
24:00	8.8	8.5	8.2	7.7
24:30	8.6	8.3	8.1	7.6
25:00	8.4	8.1	7.8	7.4
25:30	8.3	8	7.7	7.3
26:00	8.1	7.8	7.6	7.2
26:30	7.9	7.6	7.4	7
27:00	7.8	7.5	7.3	6.9
27:30	7.7	7.4	7.2	6.8
28:00	7.5	7.2	7.1	6.6
28:30	7.4	7.1	7	6.5
29:00	7.3	7	6.9	6.4
29:30	7.2	6.9	6.7	6.3
30:00	7	6.7	6.6	6.2
31:00	6.9	6.6	6.4	6
32:00	6.7	6.4	6.2	5.8
33:00	6.3	6.2	6	5.6
34:00	6.1	6	5.9	5.5
35:00	5.9	5.8	5.7	5.3

5K Pace Chart Cont.

	10000 pace	Threshold Pace	Marathon Pace
15:00	12	11.5	10.9
15:30	11.6	11.1	10.6
16:00	11.2	10.8	10.2
16:30	10.9	10.5	9.9
17:00	10.6	10.2	9.7
17:30	10.3	9.9	9.4
18:00	10	9.7	9.1
18:30	9.7	9.4	8.9
19:00	9.5	9.2	8.7
19:30	9.2	9	8.4
20:00	9	8.7	8.2
20:30	8.8	8.5	8
21:00	8.5	8.3	7.8
21:30	8.4	8.1	7.6
22:00	8.2	8	7.5
22:30	8	7.8	7.3
23:00	7.8	7.6	7.2
23:30	7.7	7.5	7
24:00	7.5	7.4	6.9
24:30	7.3	7.2	6.8
25:00	7	7.1	6.6
25:30	7	6.9	6.5
26:00	6.9	6.8	6.4
26:30	6.8	6.7	6.3
27:00	6.7	6.6	6.2
27:30	6.5	6.4	6
28:00	6.4	6.3	5.9
28:30	6.3	6.2	5.8
29:00	6.2	6.1	5.7
29:30	6.1	6	5.6
30:00	6	5.9	5.5
31:00	5.9	5.8	5.4
32:00	5.6	5.5	5.2
33:00	5.4	5.3	5.1
34:00	5.3	5.2	4.9
35:00	5.1	5.2	4.8

Half Marathon Pace Chart

TIME	1600 pace	5k pace	10k pace
1:10	12.8	12.2	11.7
1:15	12	11.4	11
1:20	11.3	10.7	10.3
1:25	10.6	10.1	9.7
1:30	10.1	9.5	9.2
1:35	9.5	9	8.7
1:40	9.1	8.6	8.3
1:45	8.6	8.1	7.9
1:50	8.3	7.8	7.5
1:55	7.9	7.4	7.2
2:00	7.6	7.2	6.9
2:10	7	6.6	6.4
2:20	6.5	6.1	6
2:30	6.1	5.7	5.6
2:40	5.8	5.4	5.3

Half Marathon Pace Chart Cont.

TIME	Half–Marathon Pace	Threshold Pace	Marathon Pace
1:10	11.2	11.3	10.7
1:15	10.5	10.6	10.1
1:20	9.8	9.9	9.4
1:25	9.3	9.4	8.9
1:30	8.7	8.9	8.4
1:35	8.3	8.5	8
1:40	7.9	8.1	7.6
1:45	7.5	7.7	7.2
1:50	7.2	7.4	6.9
1:55	6.8	7.1	6.6
2:00	6.6	6.8	6.4
2:10	6.1	6.3	5.9
2:20	5.6	5.9	5.5
2:30	5.3	5.5	5.2
2:40	4.9	5.2	4.8

Marathon Pace Chart

Time	60%	65%	70%	75%	80%	85%
2:10	8.6	9	9.3	9.7	10.1	10.5
2:15	8.3	8.6	9	9.3	9.7	10.1
2:20	8	8.3	8.6	9	9.4	9.8
2:25	7.7	8.1	8.4	8.7	9	9.5
2:30	7.5	7.8	8.1	8.4	8.7	9.1
2:35	7.2	7.5	7.8	8.1	8.4	8.8
2:40	7	7.3	7.6	7.9	8.2	8.5
2:45	6.8	7.1	7.3	7.6	7.9	8.3
2:50	6.6	6.9	7.1	7.4	7.7	8
2:55	6.4	6.7	6.9	7.2	7.5	7.8
3:00	6.2	6.5	6.7	7	7.3	7.6
3:05	6.1	6.3	6.5	6.8	7.1	7.4
3:10	5.9	6.1	6.4	6.6	6.9	7.2
3:15	5.8	6	6.2	6.5	6.7	7
3:20	5.6	5.8	6.1	6.3	6.6	6.8
3:25	5.5	5.7	5.9	6.1	6.4	6.7
3:30	5.3	5.6	5.8	6	6.2	6.5
3:35	5.2	5.4	5.6	5.9	6.1	6.3
3:40	5.1	5.3	5.5	5.7	6	6.2
3:45	5	5.2	5.4	5.6	5.8	6.1
3:50	4.9	5.1	5.3	5.5	5.7	6
3:55	4.8	5	5.2	5.4	5.6	5.8
4:00	4.7	4.9	5	5.2	5.5	5.7
4:10	4.5	4.7	4.8	5	5.2	5.5
4:20	4.3	4.5	4.7	4.8	5	5.3
4:30	4.2	4.3	4.5	4.7	4.9	5.1
4:40	4	4.2	4.3	4.5	4.7	4.9
4:50	3.9	4	4.2	4.3	4.5	4.7
5:00	3.7	3.9	4	4.2	4.4	4.6

Marathon Pace Chart Cont.

Time	90%	95%	100%	105%	110%	115%	120%
2:10	11	11.5	12.1	12.7	13.4	14.1	14.8
2:15	10.6	11.1	11.6	12.2	12.9	13.6	14.4
2:20	10.2	10.7	11.2	11.8	12.4	13.2	14
2:25	9.9	10.3	10.8	11.4	12.1	12.7	13.5
2:30	9.5	10	10.5	11	11.6	12.3	13.1
2:35	9.2	9.7	10.1	10.7	11.3	12	12.7
2:40	8.9	9.4	9.8	10.3	10.9	11.5	12.3
2:45	8.7	9.1	9.5	10.1	10.6	11.2	11.9
2:50	8.4	8.8	9.2	9.7	10.3	10.9	11.6
2:55	8.2	8.6	9	9.5	10	10.6	11.2
3:00	7.9	8.3	8.7	9.2	9.7	10.2	10.9
3:05	7.7	8.1	8.5	8.9	9.4	10	10.6
3:10	7.5	7.9	8.3	8.7	9.2	9.8	10.3
3:15	7.3	7.7	8.1	8.5	9	9.5	10.1
3:20	7.1	7.5	7.9	8.3	8.7	9.2	9.8
3:25	7	7.3	7.7	8.1	8.5	8.9	9.5
3:30	6.8	7.1	7.5	7.9	8.3	8.8	9.4
3:35	6.6	7	7.3	7.7	8.1	8.6	9.1
3:40	6.5	6.8	7.1	7.5	7.9	8.4	8.9
3:45	6.4	6.7	7	7.3	7.8	8.2	8.7
3:50	6.2	6.5	6.8	7.2	7.6	8	8.5
3:55	6.1	6.4	6.7	7	7.4	7.8	8.3
4:00	6	6.2	6.6	7.1	7.3	7.7	8.2
4:10	5.7	6	6.3	6.6	7	7.4	7.8
4:20	5.5	5.8	6.1	6.4	6.7	7.1	7.6
4:30	5.3	5.5	5.8	6.1	6.5	6.9	7.3
4:40	5.1	5.4	5.6	5.9	6.2	6.6	7
4:50	4.9	5.2	5.4	5.7	6	6.4	6.6
5:00	4.8	5	5.3	5.5	5.8	6.2	6.5

MEET THE AUTHOR

AMY BEATTY is a treadmill enthusiast. A former Division I NCAA Collegiate track and cross country runner, Beatty utilized treadmill training to prepare her for the NCAA Championships 10,000 meter race. She continues to turn to the treadmill while training for marathons and endurance triathlons. With seventeen years of treadmill training under her belt, Beatty has managed to only fall off the treadmill once. Amy Beatty is a long distance runner, triathlete, CrossFit enthusiast, ACSM Personal Trainer and Certified Spinning Instructor.

For additional treadmill workouts (new workouts added every week), visit *www.ChooseMyWorkout.com.*

**FIND TREADMILL WORKOUTS FOR
ANY LEVEL, ANY RUNNER!**

NEW WORKOUTS ADDED REGULARLY

OPENS OCTOBER 2015

The
BOOKFAST CLUB

You only have to read a book once, to change your life forever

VISIT THE BOOKFAST CLUB @
www.TheBookfastClub.com

You only have to read a book once, to change your life forever.

FIND YOUR NEXT FAVORITE BOOK!

What You'll Find:

- Book reviews and recommendations

- Fiction and Non-Fiction

- Giveaways

- Plus much more!

DID YOU ENJOY THIS BOOK?
If so, please be sure to leave an Amazon Review!

I'd really appreciate an honest review on AMAZON, book sites, Goodreads and/or your blog. It makes a huge difference to helping new readers discover the book. Thank you so much for your support!

-Amy Beatty, Author

ROCKVILLE
PUBLISHING

Made in the USA
Middletown, DE
12 September 2021

48141951R00080